Contents

Paul Golden

LITIGATING CONSTRUCTIVE TRUSTS

The Last Resort in Fighting Iniquity and Inequity

AMERICAN BAR ASSOCIATION

Real Property, Trust and Estate Law Section

Cover design by Andrew Alcala

Printed in the United States of America.

26 25 24 23 22   5 4 3 2 1

A catalog record for this book is available from the Library of Congress.

To my beautiful, perfect wife Keiko, our sons Benkei and Kenji, my parents Dick and Beth, and my "new" parents Kazue, Toyoo, Harry, and Teri. Thank you for inspiring me.

Acknowledgments

I would like to thank everyone at my law office, Hagan, Coury & Associates. That includes my great mentors over the past quarter century, Bill Coury and Sam Hagan, and Meaghan Keeler, who has been an extraordinary help for everything I do at work.

Thank you also to my sister Tammy for her helpful comments, to Professor James Pfander for his advice about making sure to continue to make time to write, despite the outside world, and to Paul Theroux, who made an insightful comment when I asked him about how to go about writing a book: "just do it."

About the Author

Paul Golden is a partner at Hagan, Coury & Associates, in Brooklyn, New York, and concentrates on appellate practice. Since entering law school, Mr. Golden's goal was to become New York's premier appellate attorney. His legal writings have been published numerous times, including his articles on appellate law. His articles have been cited by a federal case, legal articles, and McKinney's *Consolidated Laws of New York Annotated.* He has also given both a lecture on constructive trusts and a lecture on depositions, for attorneys' continuing legal education requirements. He has also lectured in two Japanese law schools.

Mr. Golden received his law degree from the University of Illinois Law School and his undergraduate degree from New York University. At the University of Illinois, he received awards and honors, including graduating magna cum laude and being first in his class in tort law. He has been admitted to practice in New York since 1995.

He has successfully argued two cases before the Court of Appeals, New York's highest court. In one case, the court agreed with Mr. Golden's argument, and curtailed the powers of one of New York City's administrative agencies. In the other, he convinced the court to change New

York law on a crucial issue of insurance coverage. Since then, that case has been cited more than 1,200 times by courts, secondary sources, expert opinion reports, and other appellate briefs. It was also cited by Mealey's Litigation Reports as one of the nation's ten most significant insurance coverage decisions of the year. He has argued numerous cases before New York's other appellate courts as well. One of his successful appellate cases from 2013 was the subject of a front-page article in New York's legal newspaper.

Mr. Golden also litigates a variety of commercial and real estate cases at the trial court level. Some of Mr. Golden's past accomplishments include successfully moving to dismiss a $10 million cause of action filed by a major telecommunications provider, and successfully moving to dismiss a million-dollar sister state judgment on constitutional grounds. He has won a trial and appeal, in which the court awarded his client with title to a residential building, even though his client had no recorded deed for the premises. He has also successfully moved to dismiss personal injury cases, one involving a party's death through his client's alleged negligence.

Mr. Golden's hobbies include card tricks, chess, studying Japanese, riding bicycles, and writing short autobiographies with the pretense that they were prepared by a third person.[1]

Paul Golden can be reached at Hagan, Coury & Associates, 908 Fourth Avenue, Brooklyn, NY. (Phone is 718-788-5052; email is prgolden@aol.com.)

1. Apologies to Steve Martin, as this is a joke borrowed from the inside flap of "Cruel Shoes."

Introduction

Although this is not a novel, the subject matter of the book is fiction—a legal fiction created by judges. The fictional concept is that someone who stabbed his former best friend in the back, and took away his property, is actually now holding that property, as a trustee, and "in trust" for his former friend, who is now the beneficiary.

A traditional express trust is planned out by the people involved, who decide everything ahead of time, including who will be the trustee and who will be the beneficiary. But a constructive trust is one created by the judge,[1] who puts people in those roles. Ironically, he puts the trustee in a role he never would expect to have, and certainly would not want to have. Not only that, but his role is then backdated, as if he had been a trustee from the date he originally got the property. If that were not bad enough, he does not even get to enjoy that role,

---

1. There is another way of looking at how a constructive trust comes into being. "It is an elementary mistake to suppose that a court creates the trust. The expression 'the court constructs the trust' is 'absurd.'" The court indicated that the trust is "imposed by law" and created once the backstabber receives the property. U.S. v. $4,224,958.57, 392 F.3d 1002, 1004 (9th Cir. 2004) (citation omitted).

because he must immediately hand the property over to the beneficiary, as well as any profits he may have made on it.

Constructive trusts are "an equitable remedy devised to prevent unjust enrichment and compel restitution of property that in equity and good conscience does not belong to the Defendant."[2] King Lear, who transferred his whole kingdom to ungrateful daughters, should have hired an attorney to try to recover it, using a constructive trust theory.

The first Restatement of Restitution, published in 1937, embodies the general principle for all kinds of constructive trusts. Section 160 states that "[w]here a person holding title to property is subject to an equitable duty to convey it to another on the ground that he would be unjustly enriched if he were permitted to retain it, a constructive trust arises."

Traitorous partners, gold-digging girlfriends, old ladies being tricked out of preparing a fair will, and plain old murder. These have been, and will continue to be, the subjects of constructive trusts. The facts in some constructive trust cases are so outrageous, one often feels like a voyeur, but without the shame.

A constructive trust is an amazing tool to avoid such issues as the statute of frauds; one can potentially obtain an interest in real property based in part on oral conversations. A plaintiff with a successful constructive trust case can also move to the head of the line in the event the

---

2. Amdura Nat'l Distrib. Co. v. Amdura Corp., Inc. (*In re* Amdura Corp.), 75 F.3d 1447, 1451–52 (10th Cir. 1996) (internal quotation marks and citation omitted).

defendant lacks assets to pay all of his creditors. One can avoid the effect of the homestead law as well. Equitable considerations, and not necessarily exacting guidelines about meeting certain elements reserved for traditional causes of action, rule the day.

It's also an underused tool to avoid losing a case through summary judgment; the constructive trust case is sometimes the sole surviving cause of action, when all else fails. In fact, at least one state[3] has indicated that it is the last resort, and that a constructive trust is only available where the wrong "cannot be addressed under other legal theories."[4]

These great benefits come at a serious price. A primary one is the heavy burden of proof. Yet, depending on the relationship between the parties, these burdens may be simple to overcome.

Constructive trusts represent one of the ultimate balancing acts. On the one hand, society needs specifics about when someone has crossed the line and has taken something they are not entitled to. More critically, in the context of real property, hundreds of years of precedent indicate that no one can claim that they were given an interest in real property without a signed writing to that effect. On the other hand, judges wish to provide equity, and if they believe someone has been taken advantage of, and had their property taken in a way that does not fit any traditional tort, then a constructive trust can come to the rescue.

---

3. Jordan v. Hagler, 179 S.W.3d 217, 220 (Tex. App.—Fort Worth 2005) (italics omitted).

4. It reminds one of the old Federal Express tagline—"When it absolutely, positively has to be there overnight."

In the event a reader wonders why Louisiana law does not show up in this book, the answer is simple. Louisiana apparently does not support the constructive trust theory.[5] This is likely one of many reasons this book will not wind up in many Louisiana law firms or law school libraries.

5. Its lower appellate courts have been generally hostile to the concept. See, e.g., Succession of Gaston v. Koontz, 49 So. 3d 1054, 1058 (La. App. 2010) ("While many other states recognize constructive trusts, Louisiana does not."); Schwegmann v. Schwegmann, 441 So. 2d 316, 322–23 (La. App. 1983) ("[I]t is clear the Louisiana Civil Code prohibits the imposition of a constructive trust on property."); Plaquemines Parish Comm'n Council v. Delta Dev. Co., 486 So. 2d 129, 135 (La. App. 1986) ("While the constructive trust theory has appeal as a means to chastise an unfaithful fiduciary, it is anathema to civilian notions of ownership, a precept unsupported by the Civil Code.") rev'd on other grounds, Plaquemines Parish Comm'n Council v. Delta Dev. Co., 502 So. 2d 1034 (La. 1987).

Chapter 1

The Basics

A. The Origin of Constructive Trusts

The constructive trust theory of law has its origins in slavery and the bursting of an economic bubble.

The South Sea Company was formed in 1711 in London; its goal was to supply 4,800 slaves a year, for a total of 30 years, to certain plantations in central and southern America. Evidently, few could resist the thrill of this kind of investment. But then the company's stock reached a height that its economics could not bear, and in 1720 the value of the shares collapsed. Huge numbers of people lost their life savings, high-ranking politicians were disgraced, and some people who had allegedly profited immorally from the company had their assets confiscated. Robert Walpole, considered England's first prime minister, came to power in the wake of the various resignations.

In this new clean era, an appellate court called the Exchequer Court heard the case *Keech v. Sandford,* which is considered one of the first cases concerning a fiduciary. It is also considered one of the first cases involving a constructive trust.[1]

In that case, the defendant was a trustee for a trust that benefited a minor. The trust property included a lease for space in an open market called Romford Market near London. The landlord refused to renew the lease. However, the defendant, presumably believing that any tenant in that space would make a profit, entered into his own deal with the landlord, and had a lease issued to himself. The minor filed an action against the defendant, and the court recognized that the defendant had not technically committed any fraud. Nor did the court indicate that there was any preexisting law that would bar the defendant from making his own deal. In fact, the court held that when the landlord would not renew the lease with the trust, anyone else on planet earth could have entered a lease with the landlord without having done anything wrong. However, the court held that a fiduciary such as a trustee had a special relationship that barred him from obtaining that lease.

The court held that the trustee's actions were inappropriate, perhaps thinking that due to (then) current events, the basis for its decision was clear enough. As one New York court put it, "The object of the rule which precludes trustees from dealing for their own benefit, in

1. 25 Eng. Rep. 223 (Ch. 1726).

matters to which their trust relates, is to prevent secret frauds by removing all inducement to attempt them."[2]

Perhaps the most interesting aspect of *Keech* is the relief the court awarded. The court, using the concept of a constructive trust, held that the lease should now be assigned to the minor, and that the trustee would have to provide to the infant an accounting of the profits he had made thus far from that lease. This is despite the fact that the court did not rule that the new lease was literally part of the existing trust. If it had been part of the existing trust, and the fiduciary had kept those funds, the result would have been obvious. But in this case, these new property rights became part of a trust, even though they were not literally a part of an existing express trust. This is, in essence, what a constructive trust is all about.

Since the time Merry Old England issued this decision, the law concerning fiduciaries and their responsibilities have flourished. And, in the past few decades, cases concerning constructive trusts have also flourished.

B. The New York Constructive Trust Theory: A Hybrid System

In order to get one's feet wet, and understand how constructive trust cases work, one method is to examine their history in one state. "[A] page of history is worth a volume of logic."[3] As noted by Judge Oliver Wendell Holmes, "[t]he life of the law has not been logic: it has

2. Fulton v. Whitney, 66 N.Y. 548, 555 (1876).

3. New York Trust Co. v. Eisner, 256 U.S. 345, 349 (1921).

been experience."[4] Reviewing a number of critical constructive trust cases is also helpful to see the variety of kinds of matters in which a court will rule that relief is appropriate.

New York is a good place to begin, for two reasons. First, it more reported constructive trust cases, than nearly any other state. With apologies to James Cameron, it is one of the kings of the world when it comes to constructive trusts. Second, New York's history shows how judges struggle with the concept. New York has a standard four-prong method of defining constructive trust cases, but the courts implicitly realize that this method should sometimes be ignored.[5]

One of the earliest and most cited constructive trust cases was resolved by Hon. Cardozo. In the case *Beatty v. Guggenheim Exploration Co.*, an agent of an employer was sent to the Yukon to investigate whether it was worthwhile to obtain mining claims that were the subject of an option. While there, the agent discovered that there were other mining claims not included in the option that he believed to be essential to the successful operation of the underlying enterprise. He purchased those claims himself. Later, his employer, realizing the importance of the claims, wanted to buy them. But it was too late. So he had to seek relief.

The court held the employer had the right to demand that the agent renounce the profits of the transaction, and transfer the claims at cost. The court held that

4. Holmes, The Common Law 1 (Harvard Univ. Press 1963).

5. A third reason is that I am from New York, so my perspective is like the famous *New Yorker* cover, "View of the World from 9th Avenue."

"[a] constructive trust is the formula through which the conscience of equity finds expression. When property has been acquired in such circumstances that the holder of the legal title may not in good conscience retain the beneficial interest, equity converts him into a trustee."[6] This is one of those classic Cardozo quotes that has been cited across the country.[7]

A few years later, in *Sinclair v. Purdy*, a leading case in the area of constructive trusts (although it does not use that term), the Court of Appeals held that a constructive trust may have arisen between siblings. In order to avoid the requests of friends who desired him to post bail for them, the brother conveyed land to his sister intending that she should hold it in trust for him. But then, she would not give it back. Hon. Cardozo found it immaterial that no express promise had been made by the sister since the "whole transaction . . . was instinct with an obligation imperfectly expressed."[8] The court also held that "[i]t is not the promise only, nor the breach only, but unjust enrichment under cover of the relation of confidence, that puts the court in motion."[9]

Five years later, Hon. Cardozo resolved yet another constructive trust case called *Meinhard v. Salmon*.[10] In that one, the court held that a co-venturer breached his duty

---

6. 225 N.Y. 380, 386 (1919).

7. Not everyone was a fan of Hon. Cardozo. When he was appointed to the U.S. Supreme Court, another justice, Hon. James McReynolds, read a newspaper during the swearing in ceremony. DREW PEARSON & ROBERT S. ALLEN, THE NINE OLD MEN, 219, 225 (1936).

8. 235 N.Y. 245, 254 (1923) (citation and internal quotation marks omitted).

9. *Id.* at 253.

10. 249 N.Y. 458 (1928).

of loyalty when he extended the lease on commercial property and excluded his co-venturer from the opportunity. The court briefly touched on how the concept of a constructive trust might support relief in favor of the plaintiff. The court held that "a constructive trust is then the remedial device through which preference of self is made subordinate to loyalty to others."[11]

About 20 years later, another well-known constructive trust case was heard by the high court of New York: *Latham v. Father Divine.*[12] In that case, the plaintiffs sought relief because their late first cousin had left a will that gave almost her whole estate to defendant Father Divine, leader of a religious cult, and to two corporate defendants in some way connected with that cult. Father Divine had given himself the name "Reverend Major Jealous Divine," and his cult, called the International Peace Mission movement, grew from a small and predominantly Black congregation into a multiracial and international church. He modestly described himself as being God. (Jim Jones, who later made "drink the Kool-Aid" into a well-known phrase, was a student of Father Divine's techniques, and had his own relationship with him.) Allegedly, the late first cousin had wanted to change the will so it would no longer provide Father Divine with assets, but his disciples had threatened that cousin or otherwise found ways of preventing her from making changes.

The court held that the cousins had a potentially valid cause of action, ruling that "[a] constructive trust will be erected whenever necessary to satisfy the demands

11. *Id.* at 467.
12. 299 N.Y. 22 (1949).

of justice. Since a constructive trust is merely the formula through which the conscience of equity finds expression, its applicability is limited only by the inventiveness of men who find new ways to enrich themselves unjustly by grasping what should not belong to them."[13]

A few decades later, in a Court of Appeals case resolved in 1976, *Sharp v. Kosmalski*,[14] the plaintiff was a 56-year-old farmer, whose wife of 32 years had just died. He had little education, and then developed a very close relationship with defendant, a potential trophy wife. She was a school teacher, and 16 years younger than the farmer. As time went on, he proposed to her, but she rebuffed him. (Presumably, this is the way gold diggers handle their men; they refuse an initial offer of engagement, in the hope they will get bigger and better offers.) He fell for it, giving her many gifts, access to his bank account, and ultimately transferring to her virtually all of his property, including his farm. Then, as a major shock to the farmer (but probably no one else) she suddenly ended their relationship and ordered him to move out of her new house and farm. He was left with nothing but the bankruptcy barrel and suspenders.

In that case, the Court of Appeals formalized the basic elements of a constructive trust, which lower appellate courts had been describing. It indicated that for a constructive trust case, the following four requirements must be present: (1) a confidential or fiduciary relation, (2) a promise, (3) a transfer in reliance thereon, and (4) unjust enrichment. In New York, this is a critical

13. *Id.* at 27.
14. 40 N.Y.2d 119 (1976).

four-prong test. It then held that all of these elements were met by the pleadings. For example, although there was no literal promise that he would be permitted to remain on the farm for the rest of his life, there was an implicit one.

Two years later, the Court of Appeals resolved another constructive trust case called *Simonds v. Simonds*,[15] which seemed to ease off the rule that only the four-prong theory applied. In that case, the plaintiff was the decedent's first wife, and sought a constructive trust on proceeds of insurance policies on decedent's life. She claimed that even though the policies were in favor of her late husband's second wife and daughter, she had a superior equitable interest arising out of a provision in her separation agreement with her late husband, which required him to continue naming her as a beneficiary even if the policies lapsed. The court held that such relief was possible even if it did not follow the four-prong theory, noting that in the *Latham v. Father Divine* case, the constructive trustee had no confidential or fiduciary relation, there was no promise by the trustee, and there was no transfer in reliance by the late husband. The court also indicated, perhaps as an aside, that one could argue that all prongs were met in this insurance case.[16] (A later case from 1984 indicated that a decedent's first wife could be entitled to similar relief even if the separation agreement did not specify an obligation to renew policies for the first wife.[17])

15. 45 N.Y.2d 233 (1978).
16. *Id.* at 236–37.
17. Rogers v. Rogers, 63 N.Y.2d 582, 586 (1984).

In 1980, however, the court further backed off from putting every conceivable action into the constructive trust basket. In *Bankers Security Life Insurance Society v. Shakerdge*, also concerning an insurance policy, the decedent's brother was a named beneficiary. The decedent had married about 13 months before he died, but he had not changed the named beneficiary. At best, the decedent's brother had made a promise that he would "do the right thing" and "take care of" decedent's wife and child. That was not enough of a promise to impress a constructive trust.[18]

In 1984, the Court of Appeals indicated there were further limits on establishing a constructive trust. In *Scivoletti v. Marsala*, the owner of the premises used her own assets to purchase the home, but allowed family members to live there.[19] The family members paid off part of the mortgage, and at least one family member had an expectation that he would wind up with part ownership. When he didn't, his widow sought relief. The lower court held there were two problems: (1) the plaintiffs never owned the premises in the first place, so there was no "transfer," and (2) there was no implicit or explicit promise. The Court of Appeals affirmed, but just focused on the lack of a promise.

For unknown reasons, since 1984, the Court of Appeals has not made any substantive or memorable decisions about the elements of a constructive trust case, possibly because it believes New York law has been fully

18. 49 N.Y.2d 939, 940 (1980).
19. 61 N.Y.2d 806 (1984).

explained for the appellate courts. Or possibly starting from scratch may become overly burdensome. Or perhaps the court believes there are more critical issues to resolve.

Regardless, New York lower courts constantly hear constructive trust cases. And for those who enjoy reading about celebrities and their problems, the rapper Curtis "50 Cent" Jackson once faced a constructive trust case filed by Shaniqua Tompkins, his ex-girlfriend (and mother of his child). He had allegedly promised to take care of her for the rest of her life if he ever made it big in the entertainment industry. The motion papers in that case show a real Rashomon story; their points of view about promises and the true nature of their relationship are completely different. She says she paid for his tattoos, a diamond ring, and a watch, which were necessary for him to be a "real" rapper, and that she helped him recover after he was nearly fatally shot. He says that she was just his baby's mother. But there was no dispute that (1) they never not get married, (2) they had no written contract, and (3) at some point the relationship soured.

One of her claims was for an interest in the home she allegedly helped to select and negotiate the price for. Mr. Cent had allegedly told her many times that he would put it in her name. He even sent her an email that read, "Neek it realy hert me to hear you say you think I wouldn't Take care of you. . . . You can have the house I'll have them put it in your name And I will give you money every month it dosent matter to me."[20] But when

20. He is known for his performances as a rapper, and not in spelling bees.

push came to shove, he did not give her the house. In any event, the court ruled that she had not contributed any effort or money toward the purchase, maintenance, or improvement of the home. Shopping for real estate and possibly negotiating its price was not sufficient for a constructive trust cause of action.[21]

Even though New York has had a great number of constructive trust cases, its primary method of classifying them is dated, artificial, and limited. It still often only relies on a four-prong test concerning a breach of a fiduciary duty. New York judges sometimes say if it does not fit into that narrow box, it is not a constructive trust. But there are a number of times in which even New York courts indicate that there are many exceptions to the four-prong test.

Florida and Mississippi have also sometimes indicated that the same four-prong test is appropriate,[22] but other states have a much different method of determining whether a party has a true constructive trust. They do not rule that the four-prong test is the only way of resolving the matter, because it is not.

Sometimes New York judges seem to have a bias against constructive trust cases. In those cases, the courts go back to the four prongs, not recognizing that there are numerous exceptions to the four-prong test, and that many cases indicate not all are required. A defendant in

---

21. Tompkins v. Jackson, 2009 N.Y. Slip Op. 50319, 17–18 (N.Y. Sup. Ct. 2009). The court decision noted that during the pendency of the case, while his ex was still living there, the house was "destroyed by a fire (deemed suspicious by authorities)."

22. Abele v. Sawyer, 750 So.2d 70, 74 (Fla. Dist. Ct. App. 1999); Carlson v. Brabham, 199 So.3d 735, 744 (Miss. Ct. App. 2016).

such a case has to use all of his powers to argue that the four prongs are a solid absolute; the plaintiff will either try to make the spare peg fit in the round hole or will point out the many exceptions.

C. The Two Varieties of Constructive Trust Cases

New York's vision of constructive trust cases is stilted. Viewing all constructive trust cases first through the lens of four-prong test, and then determining whether there are certain limited exceptions, is not the best way of understanding them.

A more appropriate way of viewing constructive trust cases is that they come in two general classes.[23] One is the New York four-prong category, that is, that one party had transferred property to a fiduciary, after the fiduciary made an explicit or implicit promise to allow the first party to reap benefits. That category is described in Chapter 2. But the other kind is that a defendant committed a kind of wrong or tort against the plaintiff, and that equity calls out to have certain assets transferred to the plaintiff due to those actions. That is described in Chapter 3. (There are other ways of breaking it down; for example, Tennessee courts indicate that there are four types of cases warranting a constructive trust.[24] But for the purposes of this book, it would be most effective to consider two types.)

---

23. *See* Charles Hester Enters, Inc. v. Ill. Founders Ins. Co., 114 Ill. 2d 278, 293 (1986).

24. Myers v. Myers, 891 S.W.2d 216, 219 (Tenn. Ct. App. 1994).

Although most states rely on case law to determine what is described as a constructive trust, this is not universal. For example, in California, the principal constructive trust situations are set forth in its Civil Code. Section 2223 provides that "[o]ne who wrongfully detains a thing is an involuntary trustee thereof, for the benefit of the owner." Section 2224 provides that "[o]ne who gains a thing by fraud, accident, mistake, undue influence, the violation of a trust, or other wrongful act, is, unless he has some other and better right thereto, an involuntary trustee of the thing gained, for the benefit of the person who would otherwise have had it." That broad definition covers both of the two general varieties of constructive trust: (1) the "transfer to fiduciary," and (2) the wrongful act.

Chapter 2

The First Kind of Constructive Trust: "Transfer to Fiduciary" Variety

As indicated in Chapter 1, if one breaks down constructive trusts into two varieties, one type concerns a transfer to a fiduciary, or a confidential relationship breach. This is the variety that New York was describing when it proposed the four-prong test: (1) a confidential or fiduciary relation, (2) a promise, (3) a transfer in reliance thereon, and (4) unjust enrichment. A description of the first three elements follows in this chapter. (The last prong, unjust enrichment, applies to all constructive trusts, and it is described in Chapter 4.)

A. Confidential Relationship

The presence of a confidential relationship is not a necessary element of a constructive trust, "although its presence makes it easier for one to be imposed."[1]

In the context of a constructive trust based on the breach of a fiduciary relationship, one must first understand what qualifies as such a relationship. Parties have a fiduciary relationship "when one of them is under a duty to act for or to give advice for the benefit of another upon matters within the scope of the relation."[2] As another court put it, "[a] constructive trust will be imposed only when it appears that the parties are in fact in a confidential relationship with one party enjoying an advantage over the other because of superior knowledge or influence and that this domination caused a gift to entireties property to arise."[3]

There are at least two types of fiduciary relationships: (1) a formal fiduciary relationship arising as a matter of law, such as between partners or an attorney and a client, and (2) an informal or confidential fiduciary relationship arising from a moral, social, domestic, or merely personal relationship where one person trusts in and relies upon another.[4] Another court agreed that there

---

1. U.S. for Use and Benefit of Allied Bldg. Products Corp. v. Federal Ins. Co., 729 F. Supp. 477, 478 (U.S. Dist. Md. 1990).

2. EBC I, Inc. v. Goldman Sachs & Co., 5 N.Y.3d 11, 19 (2005), quoting RESTATEMENT (SECOND) OF TORTS § 874, cmt. a.

3. Butler v. Butler, 464 Pa. 522, 529 (Pa. 1975).

4. Crim Truck & Tractor v. Navistar Int'l Transp. Corp., 823 S.W.2d 591, 594 (Tex. 1992); Smith v. Deneve, 285 S.W.3d 904, 911 (Tex. App.—Dallas 2009, no pet.).

were two varieties of fiduciary relationships, but broke them down differently. In the first, one party is under the domination of another. In the second, circumstances justify a party's belief that his or her welfare or instructions will guide the other's actions.[5]

In most cases concerning a breach of fiduciary relationship there must be "a relationship of blood, business, friendship, or association in which the parties reposed special trust or confidence in each other and were in a position to have and exercise influence over each other and in which one party relied on the good faith of another to his or her detriment."[6] The courts repeatedly advise that such a relationship, as a touchstone for fiduciary liability, is fact-specific, and must be decided based on the factual circumstances alleged.[7] A familial relationship, while considered a factor, does not by itself establish a fiduciary relationship.[8] Neither is simply knowing a person for a long time and trusting them sufficient.[9] Rather, a more effective claim would be that one relied on another's superior expertise or knowledge.[10]

The factors to be considered in determining the existence of a fiduciary or confidential relationship are

---

5. *See* Wimmer v. Wimmer, 287 Md. 663, 668–69 (1980).

6. Brown v. Foulks, 232 Kan. 424, 432 (1983).

7. Recant v. N.Y. Presbyt. Hosp., 25 Misc.3d 1219 (A) (Sup. Ct. N.Y. Cnty. 2009).

8. Uddo v. DeLuca, 425 F. Supp. 3d 138, 155 (E.D.N.Y. 2019); Kilpatrick v. Kilpatrick, No. 02-12-00206-CV (Tex. App. July 25, 2013); Liapis v. 2d Jud. Dist. Ct. of State, 282 P.3d 733, 738 (Nev. 2012).

9. Kallman v. Pinecrest Modular Homes, Inc., 81 A.D.3d 692 (N.Y. App. Div. 2011).

10. *See* Chasanoff v. Perlberg, 19 A.D.3d 635 (N.Y. App. Div. 2005).

the degree of kinship of the parties; the disparity in age, health, mental condition, education, and business experience between them; and the degree of trust placed in the dominant party.[11]

A confidential fiduciary relationship may exist where influence has been acquired and abused or where confidence has been reposed and betrayed.[12] Whether a confidential relationship exists is determined from the actualities of the relationship between the persons involved.[13]

Many courts recognize that even informal relationships may give rise to a fiduciary duty. "Such informal fiduciary relationships have also been termed 'confidential relationships' and may arise where one person trusts in and relies upon another, whether the relation is a moral, social, domestic or merely personal one."[14]

Not all fiduciary relationships are those between relatives, or other personal relationships. They can also arise in business contexts. For example, fiduciary relationships may also arise from contractual relationships involving joint business enterprises, or where one party has superior knowledge and the other party relies on him.[15] A fiduciary relationship may exist between partners, or between the

---

11. Kester v. Crilly, 405 Ill. 425, 432 (1950).

12. 823 S.W.2d at 594.

13. Thigpen v. Locke, 363 S.W.2d 247, 253 (Tex. Civ. App. 1962).

14. 823 S.W.2d at 594 superseded by statute on other grounds as noted in Subaru of Am., Inc. v. David McDavid Nissan, Inc., 84 S.W.3d 212, 225–26 (Tex. 2002) (citation and certain internal quotation marks omitted).

15. Wolf v. Brungardt, 215 Kan. 272 (1974).

widow of a deceased partner and the surviving partner.[16] Such a relationship may exist between joint venturers in a business enterprise.[17] The officers and directors of a corporation occupy a strict fiduciary relationship with respect to both the corporation and its shareholders.[18] On the other hand, some courts hold there is no fiduciary duty covering business dealings between businessmen: "[s]ubjective business trust, cordiality and the trust which prevails between businessmen which is the foundation of ordinary contract law" is not a basis for imposing a trust that would thwart the statute of frauds.[19] Also, people who merely conduct arm's-length transactions do not have such a relationship.[20]

When one wants to claim a fiduciary relationship between businessmen, one has special challenges. For example, in the case *Consolidated Gas Equipment Co. v. Thompson*,[21] the Supreme Court of Texas held that no constructive trust was created under Texas law between businessmen, because the parties did not meet a requirement of dealings "over a long period of time, [where] the parties had worked together for the joint acquisition and development of property previous to the particular agreement sought to be enforced."[22] Stating that there was no

16. 232 Kan. 424 (Kan. 1983).

17. Paul v. Smith, 191 Kan. 163 (Kan. 1963); 232 Kan. 424.

18. Newton v. Hornblower, Inc., 224 Kan. 506 (1978).

19. Rankin v. Naftalis, 557 S.W.2d 940, 944 (Tex. 1977).

20. *See* Williams v. Dresser Indus., Inc., 120 F.3d 1163, 1168 (11th Cir. 1997).

21. 405 S.W.2d 333 (Tex. 1966).

22. *Id.* at 337.

prior fiduciary relationship between the parties, the court refused to invoke the remedy of a constructive trust. The court recognized "the fact that one businessman trusts another, and relies upon his promise to carry out a contract, does not create a constructive trust. To hold otherwise would render the Statute of Frauds meaningless."[23] (See also *Foxley v. Sotheby's Inc.*[24]—"Generally, a special relationship requires prior or ongoing interaction. An arm's length business relationship is not enough.")

Especially in the context of a business relationship, an attorney must be able to plead with detail why there could possibly be a fiduciary relationship. The mere allegation of a fiduciary relationship in such a context will not be sufficient.[25]

As a reminder, one cannot simply hope to disprove a confidential relationship and thereby necessarily defeat a constructive trust case. If the case does not fall under the "confidential relationship breach" variety, then a confidential relationship issue has no relevance. For example, in one case, the decedent's heirs-at-law prevented her from executing a will leaving her estate to a friend. The Texas Supreme Court held that a constructive trust could apply, and there was no need to establish a special trust or fiduciary relationship between the intended beneficiary and the heirs-at-law.[26]

---

23. *Id.* at 336.

24. 893 F. Supp. 1224, 1232 (S.D.N.Y. 1995).

25. *See* Osan Ltd. v. Accenture LLP, 454 F. Supp. 2d 46, 57 (E.D.N.Y. 2006).

26. Pope v. Garrett, 147 Tex. 18 (1948).

B. Transfer in Reliance

New York and Florida indicate that one of the elements of a constructive trust is that the property must have been "transferred in reliance" on the promise. (As it turns out, there are bases for a constructive trust, as indicated later in this book, without that element.) But some other cases outside those states also refer to the same standard.[27] Although it may sound like just one issue, there are two at stake: both the transfer and the reliance. This has been given a little less attention than other issues.

One tricky example includes *Palazzo v. Palazzo*,[28] in which a married couple had a joint account, and the husband removed what he considered "his" portion of the funds, to purchase property in his own name. When she filed a divorce action, the court held that this was at least partially a transfer of "her" money, and therefore she was entitled to a constructive trust.

The case *Christou v. Christou*[29] is one without a transfer in reliance. The plaintiff, the wife, claimed that she had an equitable interest (but not an "of record" interest) in a bakery property. She claimed that she agreed to relinquish her equitable interest in that bakery in return for property from her in-laws, which she ultimately never received. Over the dissent, the majority held that she was not a named owner of the bakery property, so this did not involve a "transfer," and therefore there was no basis for a constructive trust.

---

27. *See* Castano v. Wells Fargo Bank, 82 S.W.3d 40, 43 (Tex. App. 2002) (citation omitted).

28. 121 A.D.2d 261, 264 (N.Y. App. Div. 1985).

29. 109 A.D.2d 1058, 1059 (N.Y. App. Div. 1985).

Another case in which there was no transfer in reliance (and therefore no basis for a constructive trust) was the case *Terrille v. Terrille*.[30] The plaintiff claimed her fiancée promised to put her name on a deed to a home in return for her agreement to marry him. Then when they did marry, he refused to do so. The court held this was not a "transfer in reliance," and that "money, time and effort alleged to have been expended by plaintiff was only that which could be expected in a normal marital relationship and was not the direct result of the promise."

C. The Transferor's Lack of a Prior Interest in the Property

Many constructive cases seek a reconveyance; Mr. A owned property, transferred it to Mr. B, and expected Mr. B to give it back someday. It is relatively clear that if all other elements can be proven, Mr. A can obtain a constructive trust relief.

What if the plaintiff never owned the asset in the first place? Few states have ruled that this fact, in and of itself, prevents a plaintiff from obtaining constructive trust relief. But New York has had a special view on this subject. This may be because it is one of very few states in which the courts can rule specifically that plaintiff must allege that the asset had been "transferred" to another. Florida seems to follow this law, but it has no apparent case law indicating that a lack of prior interest is relevant.

30. 171 A.D.2d 906, 908 (N.Y. App. Div. 1991).

Certain New York cases indicate that a "transfer in reliance on a promise" means that the alleged beneficiary must first have had a prior interest in the property. He must claim he obtained a promise that it would be conveyed back to him, and that he gave up his interest in reliance on that promise.[31]

However, even in New York, the law of constructive trusts is not limited to that situation. At least some cases indicate it also applies where the person seeking to impress the trust has no prior interest in the property, "but does contribute funds, time or effort to the property in reliance on a promise to share in some interest in it."[32] This can include payment for the maintenance or improvement of real property, or for the down payment or mortgage payments. The concept is not limited to real property. If a plaintiff alleges that he contributed his time, money, and energy into the operation of a business in reliance on defendant's representation that defendant would hold plaintiff's shares of stock in trust, the plaintiff can proceed in his constructive trust case.[33]

At least one Texas case indicated that even if a plaintiff had no prior interest in the property at stake, such as a real estate broker entitled to a commission, he could still obtain a constructive trust. In that case, a real estate

---

31. *See* Bentacou v. Goldman, 103 A.D.2d 732 (N.Y. App. Div. 1984); Scivoletti v. Marsala, 97 A.D.2d 401, 402 (N.Y. App. Div. 1983); Martin v. Martin, 169 A.D.2d 821 (N.Y. App. Div. 1991); Schwab v. Denton, 141 A.D.2d 714 (N.Y. App. Div. 1988).

32. Lester v. Zimmer, 147 A.D.2d 340 (N.Y. App. Div. 1989), cited by Henness v. Hunt, 272 A.D.2d 756 (N.Y. App. Div. 2000).

33. Matter of Bayside Controls, Inc., 295 AD2d 343, 344–46 (N.Y. App. Div. 2002).

broker was entitled to proceeds from a sale when the payment of the commission was through worthless promissory notes. A constructive trust was issued on the proceeds of a certain later sale of the same property.[34]

The Back-up Argument: Lack of "Full Payment" or "Considerable Sums"

Older New York cases take the position that if the plaintiff never owned the premises in the first place, he cannot seek a constructive trust. But newer cases do not have that kind of restriction. Most modern cases seem to indicate that so long as the beneficiary paid for the premises or for expenses on the premises after the trustee purchased it, the beneficiary may be entitled to some relief. But how much must the beneficiary have paid?

Some cases indicate that only if the beneficiary paid the full price could he seek a constructive trust.[35] The same cases indicate that if the beneficiary did not pay the full price, he can only seek an equitable lien in the premises.[36] Another old case (but affirmed by New York's highest court) indicated that a constructive trust will be imposed where property is parted with on faith of an oral or implied promise to reconvey, "but none may be imposed by one who has no interest in the property prior to obtaining a promise that such interest will be given to him."[37]

---

34. Meadows v. Bierschwale, 516 S.W.2d 125 (Tex. 1974).

35. *See, e.g.*, Foreman v. Foreman, 251 N.Y. 237 (1929).

36. *See, e.g.*, Scivoletti v. Marsala, 97 A.D.2d 401 (N.Y. App. Div. 1983); Petrukevich v. Maksimovich, 1 A.D.2d 786 (N.Y. App. Div. 1956).

37. Matter of Wells, 36 A.D.2d 471, 474 (N.Y. App. Div. 1971), *aff'd* 29 N.Y.2d 931 (1972).

In more recent years, some New York courts may have implicitly moved away from holding there is an obligation for the beneficiary to have paid the full price for premises. Some cases have indicated that the alleged beneficiary would have to prove he or she contributed "considerable sums" of money toward property after it had been purchased by the listed owner.[38] This follows some other states' case law.[39]

But if that is the test in any state, then it becomes difficult to determine when a plaintiff might have the right to claim ownership of real property that (1) he never owned in the first place, and (2) he did not pay the "full price" for. Another problem would be the situation in which a person claims to have the right to a fractional interest in real property. If the property was originally worth $100,000, and an alleged beneficiary only provided $5,000 toward it after it was purchased, does he have the right to a 5 percent interest in the property, or does he only have the right to an equitable lien (see Chapter 9) of $5,000? Does it depend on whether a court considers $5,000 to be a considerable sum? Or did the plaintiff pay a "full price" for that particular 5 percent share? If a court can award a 5 percent ownership to someone who provided a relatively small sum, it gives that party a great deal of power to be a thorn in the side of the other 95 percent owner, even though the plaintiff had no contract, and never owned the property in the first place.

---

38. *See* Depena v. Shocker, 83 A.D.3d 885 (N.Y. App. Div. 2011); Mfrs. & Traders Tr. Co. v. Berthole, 130 A.D.3d 881 (N.Y. App. Div. 2015).

39. *See, e.g.*, Lathem v. Hestley, 270 Ga. 849, 851 (1999).

Will a court wish to give plaintiffs this much power, when they have paid such a relatively small sum?

There is another tactic a defendant can take (especially with real estate) if the plaintiff never owned the property in the first place, and his improvements benefited the plaintiff as well. In such a case, the court could rule that there is no constructive trust, because the plaintiff's improvements would not necessarily be in reliance on a promise that the property would be returned to the plaintiff. For example, in *Marini v. Lombardo*,[40] the court held there was no constructive trust in favor of a husband when improvements to a property were undertaken for the husband and wife's benefit. Although these issues seem to be ones uniquely addressed only by New York courts, in the right case, a defendant in another jurisdiction might strongly consider making similar arguments.

D. Promise

In the context of the transfer to fiduciary constructive trust, a promise is generally a requirement. If no other basis (such as fraud, mistake, or coercion) fits the bill, then a plaintiff will have to do his best to prove there was a promise.

There is wiggle room. The promise does not need to be explicit; it can be implied based on the circumstances.[41]

---

40. 79 A.D.3d 932, 934 (N.Y. App. Div. 2010). *See also* Rock v. Rock, 100 A.D.3d 614 (N.Y. App. Div. 2012) (expenditures which improved the surroundings in which the claimant lived did not qualify as a "transfer in reliance" on a promise to convey property).

41. *See* Brand v. Brand, 811 F.2d 74, 78 (2d Cir. 1987).

Depending on the nature of the transaction, the mere fact that the transaction existed could be sufficient to infer that there was some sort of promise.[42] So long as the whole transaction had an "instinct with an obligation imperfectly impressed," this essentially counts as a promise.[43]

Some cases have even indicated that silence itself is evidence of a tacit promise; families do not use formal words to express themselves. One court held that "[i]n confidential family relationships, mutual understanding does not always depend upon words expressly uttered, and silence in the presence of conditional assertions may constitute tacit consent and a promise to comply with the conditions."[44] In attempting to prove that there was a promise, one can look at whether there was a part performance of it. In Massachusetts, as well, there is no need for an express promise to reconvey; even silent but implicit assent to reconvey is enough.[45] This should not be a shock; people can enter contracts in silence too. One example would be to sit at a shoe shine stand, put your feet up, and let your shoes be shined without objection. There's an implicit contract to pay a reasonable sum for that service.

Not every promise is enforceable though, even in the context of a constructive trust. For example, if the promise was made after the recipient received title to property,

---

42. Sharp v. Kosmalski, 40 N.Y.2d 119 (1976).

43. Wood v. Duff-Gordon, 222 N.Y. 88, 91 (1917) (citations and internal quotation marks omitted.)

44. Djamoos v. Djamoos, 153 A.D.2d 871, 872 (N.Y. App. Div. 1989).

45. *See* Abalan v. Abalan, 329 Mass. 182 (1952).

then that will not do the trick. The promise has to be made at or before the time of the conveyance. Otherwise, it would not make sense to enforce the promise; the concept of a constructive trust is that one was unjustly enriched when he received it. It does not matter that he received it for free, and then later made a promise to give it back, which he later broke.[46]

New York courts have required a certain "definiteness" to sustain any claims based on the promise. For example, in *Lefton v. Bedell*,[47] the court refused to find a constructive trust even though a father told his son, "this house is now yours." And in *Ogbunugafor v. St. Christopher's Union Free School District*,[48] the court refused to enforce the equivocal language—"if all goes well"—of the purported promise.

The law concerning promises can be tricky. For example, some cases indicate that in the context of real property, a constructive trust generally may not be imposed based solely on a broken verbal promise to hold or transfer the land for the benefit of another.[49] Apparently, the reason is that a mere broken promise is not fraud, or a breach of a fiduciary relationship. Therefore, it does not meet the constructive trust requirements.[50] In addition, to allow a case to proceed based on a mere broken promise would undermine the statute of frauds. However, if the broken verbal promise was (1) fraudulently made,

---

46. *See* Crockett v. Crockett, 145 Fla. 311, 199 So. 337, 338 (1940); *In re* Woolum, 279 B.R. 865, 870 (Bankr. M.D. Fla. 2002).

47. 160 A.D.2d 702, 703 (N.Y. App. Div. 1990).

48. 100 A.D.2d 580 (N.Y. App. Div. 1984).

49. Mays v. Perry, 196 Ga. 729 (1943).

50. *See* Bank v. Ins. Co., 265 N.C. 86 (1965).

(2) with the intention of being broken, and (3) for the purpose of obtaining title *in the first place*, then that could support a constructive trust.[51]

Another related critical question is what kind of evidence is necessary, especially in motion practice, to prove that the recipient never intended to perform his promise, even from the outset. (This is closely related to a topic described in Chapter 3, that is, distinguishing between a breach of contract, which does not support a constructive trust, and fraud, which could support a constructive trust.) At least one court held that a single, conclusory allegation that the recipient never intended to perform is not sufficient.[52] Of course, getting into the head of the recipient, and explaining how one can presume that he never intended to perform the promise, versus the other possibility that the recipient decided to breach it later, is difficult. It is one of those issues that often gets pushed down the road until the case settles.

One method of litigating a constructive trust case would be to "trap" the plaintiff into admitting that the alleged trustee never promised to transfer the property to the beneficiary. That can be extremely useful to ultimately defeat that plaintiff, assuming one can get that admission. It can seriously affect the credibility of a plaintiff as well. However, if a defendant can get such an admission from the plaintiff, it may be too early to celebrate. That alone may not be a basis to defeat a constructive

51. Mays v. Perry, 196 Ga. 729, 736 (1943). *See also* Griffin v. Armana, 687 So. 2d 1188, 1195 (Miss. 1996); Dowgialla v. Knevage, 48 Wn.2d 326, 336 (Wash. 1956); Kausky v. Kosten, 27 Wn.2d 721, 732 (Wash. 1947).

52. McDonnell v. Miller, 655 F. App'x 229 (5th Cir. 2016).

trust case. The doctrine of a constructive trust is not limited to a promise to transfer or retransfer property.[53] "Even without an express promise, . . . courts of equity have imposed a constructive trust upon property transferred in reliance upon a confidential relationship."[54] And the promise may be implied as well.[55]

Regardless, if the plaintiff has explicitly denied the defendant made any promise at all, it is worth a shot for the defendant to move for summary judgment. In one case, a transferor of real property sued the transferee to impose a constructive trust on the property. The court granted the transferee's summary judgment motion, because "The plaintiff was unable to produce evidence that the defendant gave him any assurances that she would reconvey the subject property to him after he transferred the property."[56]

Also, if a defendant can somehow get the plaintiff to admit that defendant did not even implicitly promise to provide the property to the plaintiff, the defendant may have a good chance of winning a summary judgment motion. In *Scivoletti v. Marsala,* New York's highest court held that "The record does not contain evidence to support a finding of any promise, express or implied, to convey the premises to plaintiff, and, consequently, a constructive trust may not be imposed."[57]

---

53. *See* Nastasi v. Nastasi, 26 A.D.3d 32, 38 (N.Y. App. Div. 2005).

54. Sharp v. Kosmalski, 40 N.Y.2d 119, 122 (1976).

55. *See* Bankers Sec. Life Ins. Soc. v. Shzkeridge, 49 N.Y.2d 939 (1980); Panish v. Panish, 24 A.D.3d 642 (N.Y. App. Div. 2005); Koslowski v. Koslowski, 297 A.D.2d 784 (N.Y. App. Div. 2002).

56. Gadman v. Catalfo, 251 A.D.2d 370 (N.Y. App. Div. 1998).

57. 61 N.Y.2d 806, 808 (1984).

Again, depending on the context of the constructive trust case, a breach of a promise may not be necessary.[58] One court noted that it is "irrelevant" whether the alleged trustee made a promise to hold the property in trust. That is because "The fact that a thief fleeing with his loot promises nothing avails him nothing. He remains a constructive trustee."[59] However, if one is going to argue that no promise was necessary to sustain the constructive trust, one may have implicitly decided that it is not the kind of constructive trust that belongs in the category of the "transfer to fiduciary" variety. It might belong in the category of constructive trusts discussed in the next chapter.

58. *See* Golden Buddha Corp. v. Canadian Land Co., Amer, 931 F.2d 196, 202 (2d Cir. 1991).

59. Kent v. Klein, 352 Mich. 652, 656 (1958).

Chapter 3

The Second Kind of Constructive Trust: "Wrongful Act" Variety

If the constructive trust at issue is missing some of the elements necessary for a transfer to fiduciary/confidential relationship breach constructive trust, the other method of proving a constructive trust is what I describe as the "wrongful act" variety. The applicable California statute indicates that a party might be deemed an involuntary trustee if he obtains the asset by fraud, accident, mistake, undue influence, or (as a catchall) any other "wrongful act."[1] Other states have similar language in their statutes. See for example South Dakota's SDCL 55-1-8, which states: "One who gains a thing by fraud, accident, mistake, undue influence, the violation of a trust or other wrongful act, is, unless he has some other and better right

1. Cal. Civil Code § 2224.

thereto, an implied trustee of the thing gained for the benefit of the person who would otherwise have had it."

Some cases have extremely broad language concerning when a party can obtain constructive trust relief. For example, one court held that a constructive trust arises "contrary to intention and in invitum, against one who, by fraud, actual or constructive, by duress or abuse of confidence, by commission of wrong, or by any form of unconscionable conduct, artifice, concealment, or questionable means, or who in any way against equity and good conscience, either has obtained or holds the legal right to property which he ought not, in equity and good conscience, hold and enjoy."[2] If a party obtains property through force, crime, or similar means, a constructive trust would also arise in favor of the person equitably entitled to the property.[3] The potential bases for a constructive trust remedy include all kinds of "wrongs." Embezzlement, conversion, misuse or misappropriation of information, and infringement of copyright are some other claims for which a constructive trust has been deemed an appropriate remedy.[4] Taking advantage of someone with a mental incapacity could also be a basis for a constructive trust.

Although there may be some cases that indicate that constructive trust cases are restricted to ones concerning "fraud" and the like, at least one case indicated that this

---

2. Zack v. Guzauskas, 171 Conn. 98, 103 (1976) (citation omitted).
3. Wright v. Wright, 311 N.W.2d 484, 485 (Minn. 1981).
4. Nelson v. Nelson, 288 Kan. 570, 589 (Kan. 2009) (citation omitted).

is a "limited view," and a "misconception."[5] Regardless, if the case concerns a "wrong" that is not fraud, undue influence, or the other more traditional kinds of bases for a constructive trust, a careful defending attorney will do his or her best to find case law that supports the "limited view."

The following sections in this chapter are some further descriptions of some of the bases for a constructive trust.

A. Fraud

There are two kinds of fraud. One is actual, and one is constructive. Either could support a constructive trust case.

Courts define actual fraud in different manners, but an obsessively detailed version is as follows: "In order to prove fraud, the following elements must be shown: (1) a representation; (2) its falsity; (3) its materiality; (4) either knowledge of its falsity or a reckless disregard of its truth or falsity; (5) intent that the representation be acted upon; (6) the hearer's ignorance of its falsity; (7) the hearer's reliance on its truth; (8) the hearer's right to rely thereon; and (9) the hearer's consequent and proximate injury."[6]

Most courts require parties to plead fraud with particularity. The more detail one can provide hitting all nine of the preceding elements, the better. One example

5. *Id.*

6. King v. Oxford, 282 S.C. 307, 311 (S.C. Ct. App. 1984).

of case law describing the particularity requirement is as follows: "[I]n pleading actual fraud the particularity requirement is met by alleging time, place and content of the fraudulent representation, identity of the person making the representation and what was obtained as a result of the fraudulent acts or representations."[7]

Constructive fraud is more likely to be a typical basis for a traditional constructive trust case, rather than actual fraud. Constructive fraud is defined in different ways, but one useful one is as follows. "To establish constructive fraud, all elements of actual fraud except the element of intent must be established. Neither actual dishonesty of purpose nor intent to deceive is an essential element of constructive fraud while intent to deceive is an essential element of actual fraud. The presence or absence of such an intent distinguishes actual fraud from constructive fraud. However, in a constructive fraud case, where there is no confidential or fiduciary relationship, and an arm's length transaction between mature, educated people is involved, there is no right to rely."[8]

Another definition of a constructive fraud is as follows: "a breach of a legal or equitable duty which, irrespective of moral guilt, the law declares fraudulent because of its tendency to deceive others or violate a confidence, and neither actual dishonesty nor purpose or intent to deceive is necessary. Two additional elements must also be proven in order to establish constructive

---

7. Terry v. Terry, 302 N.C. 77, 85 (1981).

8. Poco-Grande Invs. v. C S Family Credit, Inc., 301 S.C. 323, 325 (S.C. Ct. App. 1990) (citation omitted).

fraud: (1) a confidential relationship, and (2) a betrayal of this confidence or a breach of a duty imposed by the relationship."[9]

However, for constructive fraud, the law is unclear on pleading requirements, and there is a split of authority. Some courts require great particularity, and some do not.[10]

In any event, it is better to be safe than sorry, so a careful attorney should do his or her best to plead even constructive fraud with particularity. One court held that the particularity requirement may be met by alleging the facts and circumstances: "(1) which created the relation of trust and confidence, and (2) which led up to and surrounded the consummation of the transaction in which defendant is alleged to have taken advantage of his position of trust to the hurt of plaintiff."[11]

When trying to decide whether to plead a constructive trust case based on fraud, one should consider that there are apparently few cases in which courts have granted that relief based purely on that basis. In addition, in many states, fraud must be pleaded with particularity. To make out a prima facie case of fraud, there must

---

9. Nelson v. Nelson, 288 Kan. 570, 583 (Kan. 2009) (citation and internal brackets omitted).

10. *Compare, e.g.*, 3D Global Solutions, Inc. v. MVM, Inc., 552 F. Supp. 2d 1, 8 (D.D.C. 2008); Town of Geraldine v. Montana Mun. Ins. Auth., 347 Mont. 267, 198 P.3d 796, 801 (Mont. 2008); Mortarino v. Consultant Eng'g Servs., 251 Va. 289, 295 (1996) *with, e.g., In re* Allou Distributors, Inc., 387 Bankr. 365, 385 (Bankr. E.D.N.Y. 2008); Cendant Corp. v. Shelton, 474 F. Supp. 2d 377, 380 (D. Conn. 2007); Rosales v. AT&T Information Sys., Inc., 702 F. Supp. 1489, 1498 (D. Colo. 1988); Terry v. Terry, 302 N.C. 77, 83 (1981).

11. 302 N.C. App. at 85 (citation omitted, brackets omitted.)

be sufficient allegations of a representation of material fact, falsity, scienter, reliance, and injury.[12] One may even have to provide particular dates and times, even at the pleading stage. So a constructive trust case without fraud may be easier to get through the system.

Various cases describe the effect of a claim of fraud and whether a constructive trust will be granted. Some courts use loose definitions of "fraud." For example, in one case in Washington, the trial court had imposed a constructive trust and entered a finding that the defendant had perpetrated a fraud upon the plaintiff.[13] On appeal, the defendant argued that the trial court could not make a finding of fraud because the plaintiff had failed to allege fraud with particularity. The Supreme Court rejected this argument, stating it "is not required, in order to impose a constructive trust, that the plaintiff must prove that he was deprived of his property through acts constituting actionable fraud." The court held that it was "patently obvious" that the trial court had used the word "fraud" in "its broadest sense, as meaning inequitable or unconscionable conduct."[14]

A Kansas federal court held somewhat otherwise. In that case, defendants noted that plaintiff's claim was for constructive trust based on fraud. The court noted that in order to survive a motion to dismiss, an allegation of fraud must "set forth the time, place, and contents of the false representation, the identity of the party making the

12. Small v. Lorillard Tobacco Co., 94 N.Y.2d 43, 58 (1999).

13. Viewcrest Coop. Ass'n, Inc. v. Deer, 70 Wn.2d 290, 292–93 (Wash. 1967).

14. *Id.* at 294.

false statements and the consequences thereof."[15] The court noted that while the plaintiff may have claimed that certain assets were sold without appropriate approval, the complaint "fails to state with particularity how this amounted to fraud. The Court agrees that plaintiff's constructive trust claim is inadequate."[16]

In another federal case, the court held that when a plaintiff's unjust enrichment portion of the constructive trust claim "relies on essentially the same factual allegations that its fraud claims rest upon," the constructive trust claim is subject to the heightened pleading standard set forth in Federal Rule of Civil Procedure 9(b).[17]

Fraud versus Breach of Contract

A breach of contract claim and a constructive trust claim are oil and water. In the world of breached contracts, there cannot be an unjust enrichment, and therefore there cannot be a constructive trust. As one court put it, "[I]t is well-settled that a constructive trust does not arise simply because a party fails to perform under a contract."[18] However, a plaintiff who entered a contract, which was breached, and lost his funds or property, has at least one potential way of claiming a constructive trust. He can claim he was induced to enter into the contract based on the defendant's promise to perform and the defendant, at the time it made the promise, had a "pre-

15. Geer v. Cox, 242 F. Supp. 2d 1009, 1024 (D. Kan. 2003).

16. *Id.*

17. *In re* Prudential Ins. Co. of Am. Sales Practices Litig., 975 F. Supp. 584, 621 (D.N.J. 1996), *rev'd on other grounds,* 133 F.3d 225 (3d Cir. 1998).

18. Barriffe v. Estate of Nelson, 153 So. 3d 613, 618 (Miss. 2014).

conceived and undisclosed intention of not performing" the contract. Such a promise constitutes a representation of present fact collateral to the terms of the contract and is actionable in fraud.[19]

This is an incredibly tricky and touchy matter to allege, because the tradition is to treat anything concerning a breach of contract as unrelated to fraud; one has to be careful to use the exact proper words in pleadings and otherwise. Mississippi courts have ruled that "a constructive trust will be raised where, at the time the promise is made, the grantee does not intend to perform."[20] In Missouri, there is at least one case holding identically; if the plaintiff proves a party did not intend to perform an agreement when he made it, then there could be an oral agreement by inducement and a misrepresentation of the fact of the party's intention at the time the agreement was made, which justifies the imposition of a constructive trust.[21] However, since this kind of case is one that revolves around fraud, one must make sure to include a great deal of detail in the pleadings. A conclusory claim will not be enough.

Another example clarifies certain issues. In *Rankin v. Naftalis*,[22] the Supreme Court of Texas refused to impose a constructive trust on oil and gas lease transactions. The court noted that the parties had been involved in a joint venture. It also recognized that confidential relationships such as those in partnerships could impose a

---

19. Deerfield Comm'ns Corp. v. Chesebrough-Ponds, Inc., 68 N.Y.2d 954, 956 (1986).

20. Griffin v. Armana, 687 So.2d 1188, 1195 (Miss. 1996).

21. Wallach v. Joseph, 420 S.W.2d 289, 295 (Mo. 1967).

22. 557 S.W.2d 940 (Tex. 1977).

broader reach for a constructive trust than simple business dealings. However, the court found that the transactions in question were not based on the joint venture between the parties. It refused to extend a fiduciary duty to cover the business dealings, saying: "[s]ubjective business trust, cordiality and the trust which prevails between businessmen which is the foundation of ordinary contract law"[23] could not be a basis for imposing a trust that would thwart the statute of frauds.

B. Undue Influence

A typical constructive trust case is one in which one family member gives property to another family member. How much pressure was involved? Garden variety influence is acceptable ("Since you're a real loving father, you should give it to me"), but undue influence ("Give it to me—or else") is not. "To prove undue influence, plaintiffs must prove defendant had coercive influence on the grantor which is greater than that of a regular family relationship. Undue influence must consist of overpersuasion or coercion which substitutes the will of one person for the free will of the other."[24] Proof of undue influence requires "establishing motive, opportunity, and the actual exercise of that undue influence."[25]

Defining "undue influence" is one of those issues (like hard core pornography[26]) where you know it when

23. *Id.* at 944.

24. In the Estate of Davis, 954 S.W.2d 374, 379–80 (Mo. Ct. App. 1997) (citations omitted).

25. Matter of Fellows, 16 A.D.3d 995, 996 (N.Y. App. Div. 2005).

26. Jacobellis v. Ohio, 378 U.S. 184, 197 (1964).

you see it. One court indicated that "Undue influence is a practical, non-technical conception, a common sense notion of human behavior. . . . [C]ommon sense counsels against rigid, inflexible multi-part tests. . . . Better that the scope of equitable principles be imperfectly defined than that justice be overborne by the weight of artificial rules."[27] Another court explained that "the test of undue influence is whether the party exercised his own free agency and acted voluntarily . . . which may be determined from all the surrounding circumstances."[28]

A plaintiff can focus on a few factors to try to prove undue influence. Some examples include the mental or physical capacity or infirmity of the donor,[29] whether the donor received independent advice before making the gift,[30] whether the gift is "fair,"[31] and whether the beneficiary delayed in revealing the gift until after the donor's death.[32]

Undue influence should be pleaded with specificity; in some states without specificity in the pleading, the cause of action may be dismissed.[33]

As is true in many circumstances, reviewing cases are helpful to determine what will support a constructive trust case based on undue influence. In a jaw-dropping

27. Mullins v. Ratcliff, 515 So.2d 1183, 1194 (Miss. 1987).

28. Cersovsky v. Cersovsky, 201 Kan. 463, 467 (1968).

29. McDonald v. Hewlett, 102 Cal. App. 2d 680 (Cal. Ct. App. 1951).

30. Webster v. Kelly, 274 Mass. 564 (1931).

31. 102 Cal. App. 2d 680.

32. *Id.* at 19 (citation omitted).

33. *See, e.g.*, N.Y. CPLR 3016(b).

case, *Portland Museum of Art v. Germain*,[34] there was a question of whether Ms. Germain had used undue influence to obtain assets from the late Mrs. Potter. In that case, Mr. Potter had left all of his assets to his wife, and before he died, he asked Ms. Germain to "watch out for his wife and make sure nobody takes advantage of her." The late Mr. Potter's comments, in retrospect, were comically ironic.

The court held that a plaintiff must show that "it was highly probable that defendants exerted unfair persuasion on the plaintiff while she was (1) under defendant's domination or (2) justified in assuming that defendants would not act in a manner inconsistent with her welfare by virtue of the relationship between them."[35] "A party's weakness, infirmity, or advanced age" as well as "family relationships such as parent-child may be factored into the determination of whether there was undue influence."[36]

In that case, the defendant Ms. Germain moved in with Mrs. Potter in order to take care of her. Somehow Ms. Germain was added to one of Mrs. Potter's checking accounts, and, afterward, almost $100,000 was deposited into the account. In the same year, Ms. Germain was added as a co-owner to Mrs. Potter's certificate of deposit accounts. (By the time Mrs. Potter died, all of her funds belonged to Ms. Germain through joint accounts.) After she started working for Mrs. Potter, friends noticed paintings, jewelry, and other valuables in Ms. Germain's home.

34. Superior Court Civil Action No. CV-19-02 (Me. Super. Feb. 15, 2019).

35. *Id.* at 19 (citation omitted).

36. *Id.* (internal quotation marks and brackets omitted).

Ms. Germain also began driving a gold Cadillac that Mrs. Potter purchased for her. The next year, Mrs. Potter bought Ms. Germain a Jeep Wrangler, which Mrs. Potter had to use a stool to get into. Later, Mrs. Potter bought Ms. Germain a second Cadillac for her birthday. Even Ms. Germain claimed Mrs. Potter gifted her thousands of pieces of jewelry. Mrs. Potter also funded Ms. Germain's extensive online shopping.

If that were not enough, it was also claimed that when Mrs. Potter visited with her step-grandchildren, Ms. Germain would not leave Mrs. Potter alone with them, and Mrs. Potter did not engage in their conversations and sounded "scared and nervous" when she spoke.

Then when Mrs. Potter prepared her will, Ms. Germain appeared dissatisfied with not receiving everything. At one point, Ms. Germain complained "loudly and vociferously" about not being named in the original will. A few months later, Mrs. Potter called the attorney out of the blue, saying she urgently wanted to make changes to her estate plan. When the attorney hand-delivered Mrs. Potter's estate planning documents, Ms. Germain opened the door and, in front of Mrs. Potter, started "berat[ing]" one of the attorneys, calling one "a thief," and told him to "admit" that he was stealing funds. Mrs. Potter asked the attorney, "Why are you stealing from me?" When the attorney tried to explain that this was not the case, Ms. Germain interjected and called him a "pansy ass," claiming he forced Mrs. Potter "to sign something she didn't want when [they] asked [Ms. Germain] to leave the room." Shortly afterward, Mrs. Potter fired one of the attorneys. Her final will was prepared by a new attorney, which unsurprisingly left her entire estate to Ms. Germain.

When Ms. Germain moved to dismiss the constructive trust case through a summary judgment motion, the court held that the plaintiff had submitted sufficient evidence of undue influence to generate a genuine issue of material fact to be resolved by a fact finder, even considering the plaintiff's heightened standard of proof required by this claim.

Other case law indicates when there is not sufficient evidence of undue influence. For example, in *Miller v. Westwood,* the estate of Getty attempted to void a contract of sale in which he had consented to sell his farmland on an installment basis to the defendants.[37] The estate sought a constructive trust in part on the basis that there had allegedly been undue influence against Getty. In that case, one of the defendants had done something rare, smart, and prescient—she had tape-recorded a conversation with Mr. Getty, in which he had negotiated certain terms in his favor. Mr. Getty himself had been deposed (the original case was filed while he was still alive). He was ambiguous about the "undue influence" aspect of the case, because although he said he had been taken advantage of, he did not feel that he was forced into doing something he did not want to do.

The lower court held that undue influence had not been proven by clear and convincing evidence, and the petition was dismissed. The Nebraska Supreme Court affirmed. It first indicated that "influence" in and of itself

37. 238 Neb. 896, 906 (1991).

does not make a conveyance unlawful—there must be "undue influence."

> The Court, in examining the matter of whether a deed was procured by undue influence, is not concerned with the rightness of the conveyance, but only with determining whether it was the voluntary act of the grantor. The fact that the grantor has others who are proper subjects to receive his bounty can be considered by the court only as it bears upon the validity of the conveyance. The mere fact that there are living relatives who are denied property in favor of friends is not sufficient to set aside a conveyance. . . . [M]ere suspicion, surmise, or conjecture does not warrant a finding of undue influence, but there must be a solid foundation of established facts on which to rest the inference of its existence. This is particularly true where the parties are well aware of the existence of the contested deed shortly after its execution.[38]

The court reached its conclusion by noting that the defendants had the opportunity for decades ahead of time to pressure him, but never did so, and also noted that it appeared Mr. Getty was "intelligent" and an "independent" thinker.

There are a few lessons from a case such as this, other than to record conversations with elderly people, concerning major economic transactions. Some lessons include attempting to get a plaintiff to admit that he

38. *Id.* at 909–10 (citation omitted).

understood the transaction he was making. Other lessons include that it is critical to try to obtain evidence in whatever form concerning the plaintiff's intelligence and independence. In addition, one must also consider having experts testify about the value of property that has been sold.

C. Mistake or Accident

"In football, you get a penalty; in baseball, you make an error—whoops!"

—George Carlin, from the "Football and Baseball" routine

Despite the description of the category, that is, a "wrongful act," even a mistake or accident can be considered wrongful enough to warrant a constructive trust. One example would be if property is conveyed to someone who was not intended to receive the property. Or the conveyor meant to convey one property but accidentally conveyed a different property. Another would be if the donor mistakenly believes that the recipient is legally entitled to the property conveyed. The mistake could be mutual or unilateral.[39] A constructive trust may be used as a remedy for "innocent misstatements, or even simple mistakes."[40] And in California, the relevant statute itself indicates that a constructive trust can be imposed in the

39. Wilharms v. Wilharms, 93 Wis.2d 671, 680 n.2 (Wis. 1980) (citation omitted).

40. Flanigan v. Munson, 175 N.J. 597, 608 (2003) (citation omitted).

case of a "mistake."[41] However, the plaintiff must claim that the mistake was one of fact, and not of judgment. If it was a mistake of mere judgment, that would not warrant a constructive trust.[42]

If the constructive trust case is based on a mistake, then one should be careful to see if there are any particularity requirements for pleading issues about the mistake. One court held that "[T]he party raising the [issue] must state with particularity the circumstances constituting mistake as to all of the parties to the written instrument."[43] Certain statutes also may require particularity in pleading mistake.[44]

A defendant who wanted to claim that a mere mistake is not sufficient "wrongdoing" to warrant a constructive trust might be able to scour case law and try to find some helpful cases. But most cases indicate that "wrongdoing" is not technically a requirement for a constructive trust.[45]

An example of a mistake warranting a constructive trust is helpful to understand the concept. In one Florida case,[46] a rich man had prepared a will, and then a codicil to it. The codicil changed the identity of one of the beneficiaries: instead of beneficiary #1, now it would be beneficiary #2. Then he changed his mind before he died (it would be difficult to do so afterwards) and wanted to

---

41. Cal. Civil Code § 2224.

42. Cayo v. Cayo, 117 Wis.2d 154, 158–59 (Ct. App. 1983).

43. Best v. Ford Motor Co., 148 N.C. App. 42, 47 (N.C. Ct. App. 2001).

44. *See, e.g.*, N.Y. CPLR 3016 (b) and FRCP 9(b).

45. *See* Smithberg v. Ill. Mun. Retirement Fund, 192 Ill.2d 291, 299 (2000).

46. *In re* Estate of Tolin, 622 So.2d 988 (Fla. 1993).

revoke the pro beneficiary #2 codicil, so that beneficiary #1 would obtain benefits. The rich man was informed that if he tore up the original, like in a scene from a soap opera, that would serve as revocation. He then did that—or so he thought. He had accidentally destroyed just a copy of it. He eventually died, but apparently either did not realize he made the mistake or did not correct his mistake.

The court ruled that there was good news and bad news for beneficiary #1. The bad news was that the state law indicated that tearing up a copy of a codicil, even if done with the intention of revoking it, is meaningless. So his attempted revocation had no effect, strictly speaking. The good news was that since the testator made a mistake about whether it was an original versus a copy, this would be a solid basis for a constructive trust. Since beneficiary #2 would benefit from the testator's mistake at the expense of beneficiary #1, a constructive trust was appropriate, and a constructive trust was to be imposed on the assets conveyed by the codicil for beneficiary #1.

D. Breach of Fiduciary Duty

A constructive trust may also be applicable for a breach of a fiduciary duty, without the other elements normally required for the other kind of four-element New York constructive trust (such as a transfer in reliance). As an example, one Arizona court was faced with the following claim. The plaintiff learned that a 200-acre parcel of real property was for sale. Because he did not have the financial resources to purchase the parcel, he approached his uncle, and they entered into an oral partnership concerning taking steps to purchase the parcel, and then sell portions of it. After certain transactions were completed, and his uncle was listed as the owner of the remaining portion, the nephew asked to be officially listed as a co-owner. His uncle refused. (The uncle relied on the statute of frauds to attempt to dismiss the case, but the court denied the motion. As indicated in Chapter 7, the statute of frauds is no barrier to a proper constructive trust case.) The court held that when the uncle failed to convey a portion of the profits to the partnership or the real property to the partnership, he may have breached the fiduciary duty he owed under the partnership agreement, and therefore constructive trust relief may have been appropriate.[47]

It is difficult to know whether a case like this would pass muster in New York. As indicated earlier, New York traditionally analyzes whether the four magic prongs are met, one of them being a transfer in reliance. In this Arizona case, there was no such transfer, but other elements, such as a "promise" and the parties having a fiduciary relationship, do exist.

Even though traditionally a breach of contract case does not lead to a constructive trust case, there can be some ways around it. One example is described in the U.S. Supreme Court case *Snepp v. United States*.[48] In that case, upon accepting employment in the CIA, Snepp signed an agreement that he would not publish any information relating to the Agency's activities without first obtaining Agency approval. He breached that

47. Turley v. Ethington, 213 Ariz. 640, 644 (Ariz. Ct. App. 2006).
48. 444 U.S. 507 (1980).

contract. Over a dissent, the Court held that his profits were subject to a constructive trust. Under normal circumstances, that might be impossible, but the Supreme Court pigeonholed Snepp's behavior into the "breach of fiduciary duty" category and avoided declaring it a mere breach of contract. Another way of analyzing the *Snepp* case would be that he took information that belonged to the CIA and used it for his own purposes. That would be more in line with traditional constructive trust cases, and what actions they are designed to resolve. In any event, it might be difficult for an attorney to use this case as persuasive precedent for any other kind of case involving a breaches of contract or constructive trust. One might expect a court to hold it to be a special case.

Chapter 4

Unjust Enrichment: A Universal Requirement

To paraphrase the opening lines of *Anna Karenina*, successful constructive trust cases have one thing in common, and unsuccessful constructive trust cases are all different. The thing in common for successful cases is a valid claim of "unjust enrichment."

One court held that unjust enrichment occurs when one person obtains a benefit from another, using means such as "fraud, duress, or the taking of an undue advantage."[1] Other courts, though, hold that unjust enrichment does not require the performance of any wrongful act by the one enriched.[2] This is in part because "[i]nnocent parties may frequently be unjustly enriched."[3]

1. Heldenfels Bros., Inc. v. City of Corpus Christi, 832 S.W.2d 39, 41 (Tex. 1992) (citations omitted).
2. Lengel v. Lengel, 86 Misc.2d 460, 465–66 (N.Y. Sup. Ct. 1976).
3. Simonds v. Simonds, 45 N.Y.2d 233, 242 (1978).

"Unjust enrichment is not a proper remedy merely because it might appear expedient or generally fair that some recompense be afforded for an unfortunate loss to the claimant, or because the benefits to the person sought to be charged amounted to a windfall."[4] For example, if the claim is simply that two individuals entered into an agreement, and one breached it, that will not support an unjust enrichment claim.[5]

Unjust enrichment is also described as "the result or effect of a failure to make restitution of, or for, property or benefits received under such circumstances as to give rise to a legal or equitable obligation to account therefor."[6] Alaska defines unjust enrichment, in the context of a constructive trust, as the retention of property through "unjust, unconscionable, or unlawful means."[7]

In North Carolina to claim "unjust enrichment," a plaintiff must allege that (1) one party conferred a benefit upon the other party; (2) the benefit was not "conferred officiously, that it must not be conferred by an interference in the affairs of the other party in a manner that is not justified in the circumstances"; (3) the benefit was not gratuitous; (4) the benefit was measureable;

---

4. Heldenfels Bros. Inc. v. City of Corpus Christi, 832 S.W.2d 39, 41 (Tex. 1992) (citation and internal quotation marks omitted.)

5. Sojourner v. Sojourner, 247 Miss. 342, 353 (1963); Simonds v. Simonds, 58 A.D.2d 305, 310 (N.Y. App. Div. 1977) *aff'd*, 45 N.Y.2d 233 (N.Y. 1978).

6. Ivey v. Williams, 74 N.C. App. 532, 534 (N.C. Ct. App. 1985) (citation omitted).

7. Riddell v. Edwards, 76 P.3d 847, 852 (Alaska 2003) (citation omitted).

and (5) the defendant consciously accepted the benefit.[8] In New York, to adequately plead an unjust enrichment claim, the plaintiff must allege that (1) the other party was enriched, (2) at that party's expense, and (3) that it is against equity and good conscience to permit the other party to retain what is sought to be recovered.[9]

Some courts have their own unusual, and tougher, standards for proving unjust enrichment. For example, in North Dakota, five elements must be established to prove unjust enrichment: "1. An enrichment; 2. An impoverishment; 3. A connection between the enrichment and the impoverishment; 4. Absence of a justification for the enrichment and impoverishment; and 5. An absence of a remedy provided by law."[10] A defendant in a constructive trust case in North Dakota may be able to prove that one or more of these elements is missing, and thereby avoid a constructive trust case.

Understanding unjust enrichment is sometimes easier when one reviews a case when it does not exist. For example, if a defendant owned property to begin with, and a plaintiff made no improvements on it, then even if the defendant breached an oral promise to convey that land, there would be no unjust enrichment of the defendant, and therefore no constructive trust. Another example of a lack of an unjust enrichment (and no ability to claim a constructive trust), is if one party merely orally

8. JPMorgan Chase Bank, N.A. v. Browning, 750 S.E.2d 555, 559 (N.C. Ct. App. 2013) (emphasis and citation omitted).

9. Ga. Malone & Co. v. Rieder, 19 N.Y.3d 511, 516 (2012).

10. Schroeder v. Buchholz, 622 N.W.2d 202, 207 (N.D. 2001) (citation omitted).

promises to buy property for another and thereafter buys it for himself with his own money.[11]

A plaintiff claiming "unjust enrichment" cannot simply argue that one party was enriched at the expense of another, without more.[12] That would be mere "enrichment" without being "unjust." Instead, a benefit must have been conferred on the defendant "under circumstances which give rise to a legal or equitable obligation on the part of the defendant to account for the benefit[] received."[13]

One instructive case about unjust enrichment was from the Supreme Court of Georgia. In that case, two siblings sued a charity, and successfully argued that for technical reasons, a certain charity was not eligible to receive funds from their late mother's "payable on death" contracts, even though their late mother named that charity on the contracts. The charity counterclaimed, indicating that although it was ineligible, the late mother wished for the charity to receive those funds, and that the siblings would be unjustly enriched if they received the funds. Although the trial court awarded constructive trust relief in favor of the charity, on the grounds of unjust enrichment, the Georgia Supreme Court overruled that decision. The court held that when she improperly prepared financial instruments, naming a beneficiary not entitled to receive the funds at issue, then "the financial instruments involved here would simply become a part of her estate. Under such circumstances, any financial benefit

11. *See* Elliott v. Wood 95 Cal. App. 2d 314, 317 (1949); Salter v. Beal, 321 Mass. 105, 107 (1947).

12. McGrath v. Hilding, 41 N.Y.2d 625, 629 (1977).

13. Butler v. Butler, 239 N.C. App. 1 (2015) (citation omitted).

that the [siblings] would be entitled to receive would involve application of the laws of intestacy, not any sort of unjust enrichment."[14]

Unjust enrichment does not necessarily require the plaintiff to have suffered an injury. For example, the New York high court cited the Restatement (Second) of Agency, which indicates that an agent who acquires confidential information in certain circumstances, and conducts (for example) inside trading, then even if the principal is not harmed, the profits the agent earns in that stock transaction "are held in constructive trust for the principal."[15]

Another critical question, that confuses both attorneys and judges, is whether unjust enrichment alone would support a constructive trust case. Some courts have explicitly or implicitly held that it can.[16] Other courts have held otherwise, either explicitly or implicitly, indicating that more is necessary.[17]

Wisconsin has determined that unjust enrichment in and of itself is not sufficient to justify the imposition of a constructive trust. Its courts have decided other factors are necessary, such as actual or constructive fraud, duress, abuse of confidential relationship, mistake, commission of a wrong, or any form of unconscionable conduct.[18]

---

14. Tuvim v. United Jewish Communities, 285 Ga. 632 (2009).

15. Diamond v. Oreamuno, 24 N.Y.2d 494, 501 (1969).

16. *See* Simonds v. Simonds, 45 N.Y.2d 233, 241–42 (1978); Josephberg v. Crede Capital Grp., LLC, 140 A.D.3d 629, 630 (N.Y. App. Div. 2016); Brown v. Brown, 152 S.W.3d 911, 916 (Mo. Ct. App. 2005).

17. Gorski v. Gorski, 82 Wis. 2d 248, 254 (Wis. 1978); Steinberg v. Chi. Med. Sch., 69 Ill.2d 320, 328 (1977).

18. Connecticut Gen. Life Ins. v. Merkel, 90 Wis. 2d 126, 130–31 (Wis. Ct. App. 1979).

In short, if at all possible, a plaintiff should try to allege more than mere unjust enrichment for a constructive trust case.

Another issue is the connection between the parties. New York's high court has held that while "a plaintiff need not be in privity with the defendant to state a claim for unjust enrichment," there must exist a relationship or connection between the parties that is not "too attenuated."[19] However, that decision was purely in the context of an unjust enrichment case, and not a constructive trust case. What is not clear is how this would affect a constructive trust case. One hypothetical would be that plaintiff transferred property to defendant A and would have had a viable constructive trust case to retrieve that property. However, before the case was filed, defendant A transferred it as a gift to defendant B, who then transferred it as a gift to defendant C. Under traditional constructive trust theory, so long as no recipient was a bona fide purchaser, each potential defendant would take that property subject to plaintiff's rights. But if the court were to apply the prohibition against "attenuated" relationships (normally only applicable in unjust enrichment cases) to constructive trust cases, it could mean defendant C would be able to keep the property at issue.

19. Sperry v. Crompton Corp., 8 N.Y.3d 204, 215–16 (2007).

Chapter 5

The Additional Implicit Element: A Specific Res

A. A Plaintiff Must Seek to Recover a Specific Res

The "heart and soul" of the constructive trust theory is "Definitive, designated property, wrongfully withheld from another."[1] In other words, aside from what courts consider to be the traditional elements of a constructive trust case, such as unjust enrichment, the court must find particular property, or a res, that is the original subject of the constructive trust, or some identifiable property that can be traced back to the original res that was improperly acquired.[2]

---

1. Wheeler v. Blacklands Prod. Credit, 627 S.W.2d 846, 851 (Tex. App. 1982). *See also* Restatement of the Law Restitution § 160(i) at 648.

2. *See, e.g.*, Landers v. Sherwin, 261 So. 2d 542 (Fla. 4th DCA 1972).

If the plaintiff simply claims that the defendant has more monetary assets as a result of inequitable conduct, there is no basis for a constructive trust. If the court were to simply regard an increased value in a defendant's assets as a res, or all of the defendant's assets as a res, this would frustrate the purpose of other sets of laws, such as those that address which creditors come first in line.[3]

Although many courts indicate that the plaintiff must be seeking a specific res, even funds in certain cases may be sufficient. However, the funds would have to be specific, and in a specific location. Conversely, one cannot simply seek a constructive trust over unidentifiable cash proceeds.[4] As another counterexample of when a constructive trust is not appropriate, if the defendant wrongly obtained an overpayment of funds, and the case would otherwise fit all elements of a constructive trust, that still may not be enough. In such a case, if the plaintiff cannot specify a particular bank account in which those funds wound up, then it is not a constructive trust case. It is really one in which a party is seeking liability to pay money, which is a feature of an action in law, and not an action in equity.[5]

If the "property" at issue is money, and just money, then a plaintiff's potential right to relief can be tricky.

---

3. *See, e.g.*, Breen v. Phelps, 186 Conn. 86, 105 (Conn. 1982); 627 S.W.2d 846; Blue Cross Health Servs., Inc. v. Sauer, 800 S.W.2d 72, 76 (Mo. App. 1990).

4. Meadows v. Bierschwale, 516 S.W.2d 125, 129 (Tex. 1974).

5. Verizon Emp. Benefits Comm. v. Adams, Civil Action No. 3:05-CV-1793-M, at *7–8 (N.D. Tex. Jan. 11, 2006). *See also* Honolulu Joint Apprenticeship & Training Comm. of United Ass'n Local Union No. 675 v. Foster, 332 F.3d 1234, 1238 (9th Cir. 2003).

For example, if the plaintiff cannot allege specified, identifiable funds presently controlled by the opposing party, the case will likely be dismissed.[6] Much better would be a case in which the plaintiff alleges that the defendant somehow kept the funds separate and apart, without dissipating them.

Case law from Arizona reveals how the courts sometimes wrestle with trying to help sympathetic plaintiffs on one hand, but on the other hand trying to to comply with precedent which requires a res to still be in existence. In 1968, the Supreme Court of Arizona imposed a constructive trust despite the fact that the defendant had, long before judicial imposition of the trust, disbursed all the trust funds and closed out the account.[7] In that case, a constructive trust was possible because the court reasoned that the trust reached back to the time when the trustee was served with notice of the action. Seventeen years later, the court revisited the concept, decided it did not make sense, and overruled the 1968 case. The court held that where before judicial imposition of the trust, the party has disbursed all the trust funds and closed out the account, then in essence the plaintiff has nothing left but a general claim for money damages. That claim will not give rise to a constructive trust.[8] If there is a lesson to be learned from this, it is that if a plaintiff has any reason to believe the trust will be dissipated from the date the

---

6. *See* Eldridge v. Wachovia Corp. Long-Term Disability Plan, 383 F. Supp. 2d 1367, 1372 (N.D. Ga. 2005).

7. Markel v. Phoenix Title Tr. Co., 103 Ariz. 353 (Ariz. 1968).

8. Burch Cracchiolo, P.A. v. Pugliani, 144 Ariz. 281, 286 (Ariz. 1985).

action is filed until there is a final decision, he should try to obtain injunctive relief.

A constructive trust needs not only apply to the specific res which was originally taken. This is because a successful plaintiff in a constructive trust case wins an order requiring the defendant to transfer a like value of property in some form to the plaintiff. This applies to cash as well; even if the defendant received cash "belonging" to the original plaintiff, a constructive trust can be granted that would require the defendant to reconvey the same amount of cash to the plaintiff.[9]

B. Tracing the Res

One of the great benefits of a successful constructive trust case is that the plaintiff is entitled to priority over other creditors in satisfying his judgment from the proceeds, funds, or property. But a constructive trust is a legal fiction, based on the idea that the victim still held title to the property in question, and the defendant was holding it in trust for him. Therefore whatever property the defendant is still holding at the end of the day either has to be the original property or funds that the plaintiff "entrusted" to the defendant, or has to be traced back to that original property or funds.

If the original wrongful act concerns taking certain proceeds, but the defendant no longer has that particular property, there are two possibilities. One is that the proceeds will be deemed as having been dissipated. In

9. Lyons v. Jefferson Bank Tr., 781 F. Supp. 1525, 1530–31 (D. Colo. 1992).

that case, then it is too late to seek a constructive trust. One must simply seek a claim in law for personal liability and not for a particular res. If there are other creditors, one must just wait in line.[10] It is not necessarily the end of the world; if funds cannot be traced, a money judgment may still be entered against a defendant.[11]

The other possibility is to try to attempt to trace those specific proceeds to some sort of new res. In that kind of case, a plaintiff may have a viable constructive trust case. "[T]he rightful owner of misappropriated property or funds may trace whatever has been bought with the trust proceeds."[12] However, that money or property belonging to the defendant has to be traced to the original money or property that should have belonged to the plaintiff.[13] As one court put it, "Tracing is a process where the claimant basically must be able to point to the identifiable property or fund and say, 'This is mine.' If the funds or property are untraceable—meaning the claimant cannot determine where they were deposited or what the debtor has done with them—the equitable remedy is not available."[14] Another court explained that "It is hornbook

---

10. *See* Great-West Life Annuity Ins. Co. v. Knudson, 534 U.S. 204, 213–14 (2002).

11. Southwest Livestock & Trucking Co. v. Dooley, 884 S.W.2d 805, 811 (Tex. App. 1994).

12. Burton W. Wiand Partners v. Lee (*In re Lee*), 574 B.R. 286, 294 (Bankr. M.D. Fla. 2017).

13. Korea Supply Co. v. Lockheed Martin Corp., 29 Cal. 4th 1134, 1150 (2003).

14. *In re* Cowling, 109 Ohio St. 3d 276, 281–82 (Ohio, 2006) (citing Ashley S. Hohimer, *Constructive Trusts in Bankruptcy: Is an Equitable Interest in Property More Than Just a "Claim"?*, 19 BANKR. DEV. J. 499, 510–11 (2003).

law that before a constructive trust may be imposed, a claimant to a wrongdoer's property must trace his own property into a product in the hands of the wrongdoer."[15]

The concept of tracing is hardly new. The U.S. Supreme Court heard a case concerning victims of the original Ponzi scheme.[16] As the Court noted, Charles Ponzi had a "remarkable" career. He borrowed money, claiming he was buying international postal coupons in foreign countries and selling them in other countries at 100 percent profit. He promised in 90 days to pay his victims/investors $150 for every $100 loaned. Within eight months he took in nearly $10 million—in 1919. (As Daddy Warbucks said in "Annie" about his own first $100 million, "Boy, in those days, that was a lot of money!") Ponzi made no investments of any kind. At a certain point, he was "earning" $1 million a week, but eventually his scheme came crashing down on him.

In any event, some victims sought a constructive trust to recover from the bankruptcy estate ahead of the general creditors. They claimed in a bankruptcy case that they had a trust over certain funds. The U.S. Supreme Court held that if they had "followed the money wherever they could trace it and have asserted possession of it on the ground that there was a resulting trust in their favor" then they "would have been endeavoring to get their own money, and not money in the estate of the bankrupt."[17] However, they failed to do so in that particular case, so they were put in the general category of all the other creditors.

---

15. United States v. Benitez, 779 F.2d 135, 140 (2d Cir. 1985).
16. Cunningham v. Brown, 265 U.S. 1 (1924).
17. *Id.* at 11.

Another kind of example of when tracing is necessary was heard by the Minnesota Supreme Court in *American Railway Express Co. v. Houle.*[18] There, a husband embezzled money from his employer and used the money for the construction of a dwelling. After construction was complete, the husband and his wife lived together at the house. The employer sought, and the district court granted, the appointment of a receiver to sell the land and the house deemed held in trust for the employer. The court stated that "The rule is well established that, where a constructive trust of embezzled funds comes into being for the protection of an injured party, it is not cut off by any transfer of the property or of other property substituted therefor until such property reaches the hands of a bona fide purchaser for value."[19] The Supreme Court affirmed the district court, reasoning that "[t]he polluted funds were used in payment for work and material furnished in the construction of the dwelling, and the homestead, if such it became, would not be exempt from seizure or sale to satisfy such indebtedness."[20]

A plaintiff has to trace the end assets or funds to the original assets or funds, and many courts hold this is a strict rule. Otherwise, it becomes a free for all, and any potential plaintiff can simply plead "constructive trust" and get first in line. Most cases indicate that the plaintiff has to prove the tracing requirement by clear and convincing evidence.[21] "Unless the tracing requirement is observed with reasonable strictness, any suit on a debt or

18. 169 Minn. 209 (1926).

19. *Id.* at 213.

20. *Id.*

21. *In re* Estate of Cowling, 109 Ohio St. 3d 276, 282 (2006).

obligation could be used to impress a constructive trust on the assets of the defendant."[22]

There are at least two kinds of tracing requirements. One is "strict," and the other is more relaxed and liberal.

If the property is being held by an insolvent debtor in the context of a bankruptcy case, the court is much more likely to require the claimant to meet the "strict tracing" burden, especially in California.[23]

Strict tracing requires a creditor to demonstrate that the property subject to the constructive trust was specifically and directly exchanged for the property sought to be recognized as trust property. The rationale for strict tracing where the debtor is insolvent is to protect unsecured creditors from being prejudiced by a creditor with a similar claim from receiving priority payment from assets that would otherwise be available to all creditors pro-rata.

Under the standard applicable to bankruptcy cases involving commingled funds, the plaintiff has the burden of tracing the trust property "specifically and directly" back to the illegal transfers giving rise to the constructive trust.[24] "Such a tracing requirement is necessary to further the bankruptcy policy of equitable distribution among similarly situated creditors."[25]

---

22. Peirce v. Sheldon Petroleum Co., 589 S.W.2d 849, 853 (Tex. Civ. App.–Amarillo 1979, no writ).

23. *See In re* Goldberg, 168 BR 382, 385 (B.A.P. 9th Cir. 1994).

24. Taylor Assoc. v. Diamant (*In re* Advent Mgmt. Corp.), 104 F.3d 293, 296 (9th Cir. 1997).

25. *In re* Bullion Reserve of North America, 836 F.2d 1214, 1218 (9th Cir. 1988).

If a court does not use a strict standard, it will apply a relaxed standard. Sometimes the standard is so relaxed, that the court will imply that no tracing requirement exists at all. Just as one example, in the previously cited New York cases *Simonds v. Simonds*[26] and *Rogers v. Rogers*,[27] after a divorce, a husband was obligated to maintain an insurance policy to benefit the first wife. After the husband's death, the first wife discovered that the policy lapsed, and she sought to impose a constructive trust on the benefits issued to the second wife under the newer policy. Since the court allowed constructive trusts in such cases, this was a quasi-relaxation of any tracing requirement. That is because the new wives did not obtain the insurance proceeds from their late ex-husbands; they received the proceeds from the insurers. As the court put it in the *Simonds* case, "For a certainty, the first wife's equitable interest would be easier to trace if the new policies were quid pro quo replacements for the original policies. The record does not reveal whether this was so. But inability to trace plaintiff's equitable rights precisely should not require that they not be recognized."[28] The *Rogers* case held that "in view of equity's goal of softening where appropriate the harsh consequences of legal formalisms, in limited situations the tracing requirement may be relaxed."[29]

---

26. 45 N.Y.2d 233 (1978).
27. 63 N.Y.2d 582 (1984).
28. 45 N.Y.2d at 240.
29. 63 N.Y.2d at 586.

Another example was discussed in the case *In re Goldberg*,[30] in which the debtor received a duplicate refund of about $17,000 through the mistake of an escrow agent. He commingled the funds with amounts in existing bank accounts, and later used the accounts to make a $15,000 down payment on a home. The creditor brought an adversary proceeding to impose a constructive trust on the debtor's home and to foreclose on its interest in the property. The bankruptcy court determined that the creditor had not demonstrated direct and specific tracing of the fund to the debtor's residence. Nevertheless, the court imposed a constructive trust on the home in the amount of $15,000, because it determined that other creditors would not be prejudiced. The Bankruptcy Appellate Panel for the Ninth Circuit affirmed the decision, concluding that "it is not an abuse of discretion to allow liberal tracing when no creditors will be harmed."[31]

The concept of tracing could be one in which the defendant was "entrusted" with real property or other property, which was then sold, and the funds were put into a particular account. One could claim that those assets are traceable back to the original property. It could also work if those particular funds were then used to purchase some other asset; one could argue that this new asset could be traced back to the original piece of property.

However, many "tracing" cases concern ones in which the defendant improperly received a certain set of funds. If money is the asset on which the constructive trust is

30. 158 B.R. 188 (B.A.P. 9th Cir. 1993).

31. 168 B.R. 382, 385 (B.A.P. 9th Cir. 1994).

based, then the specific amounts must be identified and located, "either by tracing the money to a specific and existing account, or where the funds have been converted into another type of asset such as by the purchase of real property, the money must be traced into the item of property."[32]

If tracing is impossible, there is still an out. At least one federal appellate court held that where fraud is demonstrated, the court may impose a constructive trust even though the tracing requirement cannot be met.[33]

The good news about tracing property is that once the plaintiff has finished tracing it, and the proceeds are in the "hands of the wrongdoer," then the plaintiff can also recover profit or increase in value that has accrued.[34] However, in such a case, the plaintiff is limited to a proportionate interest in the proceeds, if other separate property is commingled with wrongfully taken property. This leads to the next section.

C. Commingled Proceeds

If the constructive trust plaintiff has been able to trace the proceeds somehow, he is in good shape. But a defendant at that point may have a counterargument: that the assets were placed into an account in which both the clean funds and "entrusted" funds were commingled.

32. Hanigan v. Trumble, 252 Neb. 376, 383 (1997).

33. Heyman v. Kemp.,649 F.2d 1236, 1241 (7th Cir. 1981).

34. John R. Boyce Family Tr. v. Snyder, 128 S.W.3d 630, 638 (Mo. App. 2004) (internal citations omitted).

There are least two pieces of good news for a plaintiff in such a case. First, even though the plaintiff is only entitled to the portion traceable to the misappropriated funds, the mere fact that a trustee commingled trust funds with his own preexisting funds does not prevent a plaintiff from reclaiming misappropriated funds.[35] Notably, if the original property is commingled, then a constructive trust does not need to apply to the original res. However, there still must be a kind of res.[36]

The second piece of good news for such a plaintiff is that in certain states, the defendant trustee has the burden to prove to what degree there was commingling, and what portion of the funds the defendant owned personally. This is because when trustees conduct their affairs in a manner that prevents a plaintiff from doing a precise form of accounting, the trustee, and not the trust, has to suffer the consequences.[37] If the trustee cannot prove what portions belong to himself, then the court may consider the entirety of the funds in that account as subject to the trust.[38] This would also be true if, for example the defendant trustee claimed that he used part of the misappropriated funds to purchase real property, and part of his own funds, but could not prove what part originated from his own funds. In that kind of case as well, presumably the entire real property could be subject to the trust.

---

35. *See* Variety Wholesalers, Inc. v. Salem Logistics Traffic Servs., LLC, 723 S.E.2d 744, 752–53 (N.C. 2012); Wilde v. Wilde, 576 F. Supp. 2d 598, 605 (S.D.N.Y. 2008); Keith v. Wallerich, 201 N.C. App. 550, 556 (2009).

36. *See* Restatement of Restitution § 160, cmt. i (1936).

37. *See* Tauber v. Commonwealth, 263 Va. 520, 540–41 (Va. 2002).

38. People's Nat'l Bank v. Waggoner, 185 N.C. 297, 317–18 (1923).

If there are specific funds that wind up in the hands of a defendant that would ordinarily be the subject of a constructive trust, there can be special problems if the funds wind up in a commingled account. Depending on the state and the situation, the court could determine that it has dissipated so much that it is no longer considered a specific res. Alternatively, the court could use "the lowest-intermediate-balance rule."[39] The legal fiction behind that rule is that trustees are honest, and therefore a trustee who was entrusted with funds would withdraw non-trust funds first and would keep as much of the original trust fund in the account as possible.[40]

Under that rule, if (for example) the plaintiff was defrauded out of $100,000, and the defendant put those funds into his own account, which already had $50,000 in it, for a total of $150,000, then the first funds the defendant might take out afterward would be deemed part of the original $50,000, leaving the $100,000 intact. But if the defendant took out more than $50,000, every penny more would reduce what the plaintiff could retrieve under a constructive trust theory. Amazingly, even if the defendant took out $140,000 from the $150,000, and then replaced all of it the next day, the defendant might have an argument that only $10,000 of the constructive trust would be left to be retrieved. If there is any lesson to be learned from this, it would be that a person who allegedly defrauded someone out of funds might consider

---

39. C.O. Funk & Sons, Inc. v. Sullivan Equip., Inc., 89 Ill.2d 27 (1982).

40. *In re* Charlie's Quality Carpentry, LLC, Bk. No. 02-11983-JMD, Adv. No. 02-1133-JMD, at *10 (Bankr. D.N.H. Aug. 25, 2003), citing Bogert's Trusts & Trustees (Rev. 2d ed.) § 926 (2002).

removing all money from any particular account and replacing it shortly thereafter, in order to avoid the constructive trust relief.

If that were not confusing enough, consider the rules for when a defendant takes funds from various people, and puts those funds in the same account. In that case, if multiple restitution claimants successfully trace their property back to the same commingled account, these claimants share the traced funds pro rata. All victims of the fraud may have equivalent claims, and in that case no particular victim has an entitlement to a constructive trust over the entire pool.[41]

One example of how courts resolve issues about commingled funds is the Texas case *Wilz v. Flournoy.*[42] The father used funds from his incapacitated son's account to pay the father's monthly payments on a farm. The mother presented evidence of tracing by proving that several checks were drawn on the son's account and deposited to the father's personal account, and then the deposits were used to make payments on the farm. As a result, the burden then shifted to the father to demonstrate what portion of the farm's purchase price and monthly payments came from his own funds. The father could not meet that burden, and could not prove he used any of his own funds to purchase the farm. Therefore, the court held that the son was entitled to the entire farm.

41. *See In re* Miss. Valley Livestock, Inc., 745 F.3d 299, 308 (7th Cir. 2014), citing Andrew Kull, *Restitution in Bankruptcy: Reclamation and Constructive Trust,* 72 Am. Bankr. L.J. 265, 285 (1998).

42. 228 S.W.3d 674 (Tex. 2007).

D. Specific Funds Can Be a Res

"Doublethink means the power of holding two contradictory beliefs in one's mind simultaneously, and accepting both of them."

—George Orwell, *1984*

In the context of a constructive trust case, a plaintiff cannot seek money damages. However, seeking a specific fund of money is perfectly acceptable. It is difficult to articulate why there should be a difference, but one seeking a constructive trust generally must focus on a particular piece of property, and not a fungible piece of property.

The constructive trust theory is one for equitable relief, and puts a plaintiff in a separate world, with certain benefits and certain burdens. But if one is just seeking general money damages, he will just be one in a potential crowd of others, and the plaintiff should not be given benefits such as being put at the head of the line of other creditors (at least for the res at issue).

As is indicated in Chapter 10, a critical benefit of a true constructive trust case is that it gives the plaintiff the opportunity to enjoin the defendant from spending certain funds during the litigation. This is because "injunctive relief is appropriate to prevent dissipation of specific, identifiable trust funds."[43] However, when your client is

43. Noventa Ocho LLC v. PBD Properties LLC, 284 F. App'x 726, 728 (11th Cir. 2008) (citation and internal ellipses omitted).

seeking specific funds, those funds must be ascertained as traceable to fraudulent or wrongful conduct.[44]

Before the court can impose "a constructive trust, there must be an identifiable *res* on which the trust can be impressed. If the original *res* no longer remains, but is transformed into a different form, it is the burden of the party seeking to impress a constructive trust to trace the property to specific funds before it can prevail."[45]

In order to help understand the distinction between when one can or cannot obtain equitable relief for specific funds in a constructive trust case, one can compare cases on ERISA plans. An ERISA plan is one made under federal law, which sets minimum standards for retirement and health plans in the private industry to provide protection for individuals in these plans. The portion of the ERISA statute at issue in the following U.S. Supreme Court cases allowed the petitioners to seek equitable relief (such as in the form of a constructive trust), but not for legal relief, such as money damages.

In *Sereboff v. Mid Atlantic Medical Services, Inc.*, a married couple were injured in an automobile accident.[46] They were the beneficiaries of a health insurance plan covered by ERISA, and their medical costs after the accident were covered by the plan. The plan also indicated that if a third party had caused the accident, and the beneficiaries later received money from that third party, the beneficiaries would have to reimburse the ERISA fund

44. *See, e.g.*, Bowie v. Ford, 269 Md. 111, 118 (1973).

45. *In re* Fin. Federated Title & Tr. Inc., 273 B.R. 706, 718 (Bankr. S.D. Fla. 2001), *aff'd* 347 F.3d 880 (11th Cir. 2003).

46. 547 U.S. 356 (2006).

with that money. In that case, the beneficiaries did finally settle their case against the third party, and received $750,000, but then they failed to reimburse the fund. The court awarded a constructive trust in favor of the ERISA plan because the settlement proceeds had been set aside in a specifically identified fund under the couple's control, and not in their general assets.

The U.S. Supreme Court distinguished that case from *Great-West Life & Annuity Insurance Co. v. Knudson.*[47] In *Knudson,* some of the same basic facts were the same; Knudson was involved in a car crash, the plan paid her medical bills, and then when she recovered from a third party for her injuries, the petitioner sought to collect its fair share under ERISA laws. The court held that this was not an equitable cause of action because the equitable restitution required would be one to impose a constructive trust or equitable lien on "particular funds or property in the defendant's possession."[48] That requirement was not met. The petitioner sought relief from Knudson, but those funds were not in Knudson's possession. They had instead been primarily placed in a "special needs trust" under California law. The kind of relief petitioner sought, therefore, was "not equitable—the imposition of a constructive trust or equitable lien on particular property—but legal—the imposition of personal liability for the benefits that [Great-West] conferred upon [Knudson]."[49]

---

47. 534 U.S. 204 (2002).
48. *Id.* at 213.
49. *Id.*

The Court in *Knudson* held that the participant could not be ordered to pay restitution in the form of monetary payments, because doing so would be the equivalent of granting the plaintiff compensatory damages, which is essentially a legal remedy, impermissible under the ERISA statute. The Court can only impose a remedy that was directed to "particular funds or property in . . . [the] defendant's possession" that could "clearly be traced" to "money . . . identified as belonging in good conscience" to the plaintiff. In such a case, the plaintiff's right to such property would be based on a constructive trust or equitable lien on the property. Because satisfaction of any restitution order in *Knudson* would have had to have been made from the defendant's general assets, such restitution would have been legal, and not equitable, in nature. For that reason, the Court upheld the lower court's denial of the plan's reimbursement claim. Notably, it appeared in that case that if the attorneys had sought relief against, for example, the trustee in control of the "special needs trust," the outcome would have been different.

Chapter 6

Miscellaneous Pleading Issues

A. Is a Constructive Trust a Cause of Action or a Remedy?

If a constructive trust were going through teenage angst, he might look in a mirror and say to himself, "What am I?" It's a decent question, because there is some disagreement about it. Some courts describe it as a cause of action, and some describe it as a remedy. A cause of action is distinguished from a remedy, which is the means or method whereby the cause of action is effectuated.[1] There is also a separate debate about whether the distinction is largely "immaterial."[2]

---

1. Goetz v. State Farm Mut. Auto Ins. Co., 31 Wis.2d 267, 273–74 (1966) (citation omitted).

2. *See* Tikalsky v. Friedman, 386 Wis.2d 757, 771 (2019).

In New York, most cases indicate that a constructive trust is a cause of action, in and of itself.[3] But in most other states, it is simply a remedy. One case held, for example, that "[a] constructive trust is not a cause of action rather it is a remedy that may be invoked when one party has been unjustly enriched at the expense of another."[4]

California has somewhat unclear rules. Some courts recognize that a constructive trust may be pleaded as a cause of action.[5] Other cases indicate that it is a remedy, and not an independent cause of action.[6]

In any event, if a party is seeking relief in a state that does not absolutely permit parties to plead a cause of action as one for "constructive trust," one should make sure that there are other more traditional bases for relief, and that "constructive trust" is listed as a remedy, and not simply a cause of action. As one court put it, "A constructive trust is an equitable remedy; and a request to impose such a trust is not a cause of action that will stand independent of some wrongdoing. . . . In other words, a request for the imposition of a constructive trust must be tethered to some viable underlying cause of action."[7]

---

3. *See, e.g.*, Reiner v. Jaeger, 50 A.D.3d 761 (N.Y. App. Div. 2008).

4. Freeland v. IRS, 264 B.R. 916, 924 (N.D. Ind. 2001).

5. *See* Teselle v. McLoughlin, 173 Cal. App. 4th 156, 177 (Cal. App. Ct. 2009) ("[P]laintiff could establish a cause of action for constructive trust."); *see also* Dabney v. Philleo, 38 Cal. 2d 60, 67–68 (Cal. 1951) ("[T]he complaint does allege, sufficiently as against general demurrer, a cause of action for imposition of a constructive trust [.]").

6. *See* Mattel, Inc. v. Mga Ent., Inc., 616 F.3d 904, 908–09 (9th Cir. 2010); Stansfield v. Starkey, 220 Cal. App. 3d 59, 76 (Cal Ct. 1990).

7. Keeling v. Keeling, 145 So.3d 763, 769 (Ala. Civ. App. 2014) (per curiam) (internal citations, brackets, and quotation marks omitted).

Another court indicated similarly, that "A constructive trust is a remedy—not a cause of action. An underlying cause of action such as a breach of fiduciary duty, conversion, or unjust enrichment is required. The constructive trust is merely the remedy used to grant relief on the underlying cause of action."[8]

Unfortunately, although some courts indicate that "unjust enrichment" is an underlying cause of action, and therefore a great basis to support a constructive trust remedy, other courts say otherwise. For example, in *Jogani v. Superior Court*,[9] the court held that "unjust enrichment is not a cause of action. Rather, it is a general principle underlying various doctrines and remedies, including quasi-contract." And even if one has a right to claim that a cause of action is for "unjust enrichment," one must make sure that this is not the only claim, because as described otherwise in this book, many cases indicate that unjust enrichment alone is not a basis for a constructive trust relief. (This is not universal; a concurrence in a Wisconsin Supreme Court case explained that a constructive trust is a remedy and not a cause of action, but also indicated that "Unjust enrichment is a stand-alone cause of action."[10])

If one is in a state outside New York and labels a cause of action as simply one as a "constructive trust," one may risk having the cause of action dismissed. In *Coalition Protecting Auto No-Fault v. Michigan Catastrophic*

8. Sherer v. Sherer, 393 S.W.3d 480, 491 (Tex. App. 2013).

9. 165 Cal. App. 4th 901, 911 (Cal. Ct. App. 2008) (citation omitted).

10. Tikalsky v. Friedman, 386 Wis. 2d 757, 800 (Wis. 2019).

Claims Association,[11] the Michigan Court of Appeals held that an independent action for "constructive trust" failed to state a claim and should have been dismissed. "A constructive trust is not an independent cause of action; rather, it is an equitable remedy."[12] The Court of Appeals found the trial court erred in not dismissing the "claim" for constructive trust and remanded for entry of an order granting the motion to dismiss for failure to state a claim. The only practical advice for cases like this is to try to pin a constructive trust remedy on as many potential "official" causes of action as possible. If that fails, one can comb through the state's case law, because some states, like California, have some cases indicating that a constructive trust is a cause of action, and others indicating it is a remedy.

Understanding whether the constructive trust theory is a cause of action versus a remedy is also critical in the context of the statute of limitations. Depending on what the underlying cause of action is, the statute of limitations may be different, even if the underlying relief one seeks is the same.

B. Constructive Trusts That Do Not Fit the Traditional Guidelines

Not all constructive trust cases easily fit the traditional guidelines.

11. 305 Mich. App. 301 (2014), *vacated in part on other grounds,* 498 Mich. 896 (2015).

12. *Id.* at 325.

What if your client somehow "deserved" to have the property at issue, but none of the traditional bases for a constructive trust exist? One cannot give up; if the situation is right, there still may be a chance. In *Kent v. Klein,*[13] the recipient made no promise, and no person did anything that one might traditionally call a "wrong" act, or even a mistaken act. In that case, a mother decided to divide her real estate among five of her children. Because one of her sons, John, was not well, the deed for his share was made out to a daughter, Edith. Edith had nothing to do with that decision; she apparently did not even know her mother executed that deed until after it was recorded. After John's death, Edith got tough, and refused to convey the property to John's widow and son. Yet, despite the lack of a promise, and despite not doing anything wrong at the time her late mother made the decision to have it transferred to her, the court ordered the defendant to convey a share to John's heirs.

The court held that it was "utterly irrelevant" that the defendant made no promise to anyone. The court also held it was irrelevant that there was no fraud at any particular time, and irrelevant that the property was wrongfully acquired by Edith. It was also irrelevant to analyze whether the plaintiff suffered a loss. The only issue the court held relevant was that it was "unconscionably withheld." The court, using rather dramatic and poetic language that one does not normally see in court cases, held that "[i]t is enough, to compel the surrender, that one feed and grow fat on that which in good conscience belongs to another, that he enjoy a windfall resulting in

13. 352 Mich. 652 (1958).

his unjust enrichment, that he reap a profit in a situation where honor itself furnishes rich reward, where profit, the mainspring of the market place, is both foreign and inimical to the trust reposed."[14]

The Restatement (Second) of Trusts § 45 indicates that there is yet another basis for a constructive trust, which does not seem to fit other categories: when "the transfer was made by the transferor in anticipation of death." Only a handful of states have cited this as a potential basis for a constructive trust.[15]

This is apparently not a heavily litigated issue. The rationale for the rule is a bit obscure as well. Perhaps it applies when the transferor would have wanted to hold onto his property, except that he believed he would be dying shortly. Therefore, presumably, if he survived whatever illness he thought he was suffering, he should be able to take it back. But this leads to a host of questions. For example, would it have to be in anticipation of imminent death, or just death that might occur years from the transfer? Would the transferor actually have to have lived in order to seek relief?

---

14. *Id.* at 658.

15. *See* Orud v. Groth, 652 N.W.2d 447, 452–53 (Iowa 2002); Howard v. Manes, 309 P.3d 279, 284 (Utah Ct. App. 2013); Rausch v. Devine, 80 P.3d 733, 744 (Alaska 2003).

Chapter 7

Defenses

"A technical objection is the first refuge of a scoundrel."

—Heywood Broun

A. Pleading Affirmative Defenses

Defending a constructive trust case, in comparison to winning one, is like tearing down a building in comparison to building it. First, it is easier to do. Second, it is more fun.

The first step in defending the case is to carefully consider all potential affirmative defenses in the initial responsive pleading. New York law requires parties to raise affirmative defenses that "if not pleaded would be likely to take the adverse party by surprise."[1] Some of the named defenses in the relevant statute include the

1. N.Y. CPLR 3018(b).

statute of limitations and statute of frauds. This is despite the fact that any intelligent attorney would probably not be "surprised" if one of those defenses were raised at trial, even if was not included in the answer. (In fact, the most surprising thing about a case is when a defendant does *not* include such defenses.) In Illinois, the relevant statute is similar; it requires a party to expressly state a defense "which, if not expressly stated in the pleading, would be likely to take the opposite party by surprise, must be plainly set forth in the answer."[2]

The relevant New York statute warns that "application of this subdivision shall not be confined to the instances enumerated" in CPLR 3018(b). In other words, courts can add to the list without warning, even if it is debatable and not normally considered a traditional affirmative defense. That might mean that one should raise any kind of affirmative defense wherever conceivably possible, even to the point of labeling all potential arguments as "affirmative defenses." On the other hand, it is also possible that a court could issue sanctions against the defendant who raises a non sequitur defense. This means there is no absolutely safe way to draft an answer in a constructive trust case.

Many attorneys use boilerplate language for affirmative defenses, such as "statute of limitations" or "laches." Although this may be sufficient for most judges, there are serious advantages in describing potential defenses in pleadings with some detail. For example, some case law indicates that an affirmative defense raised without

2. 735 ILCS 5/2-613(d).

backup facts or any explanation should be stricken.[3] In New York, this is due to the effect of CPLR 3018, which indicates that "[s]tatements in a pleading shall be sufficiently particular to give the court and parties notice of the transactions, occurrences, or series of transactions or occurrences, intended to be proved and the material elements of each . . . defense." In California, "new matters" need to be sufficiently pleaded to establish each element of a claimed affirmative defense.[4] Another reason to include detail is that it may help in negotiations when the plaintiff realizes that his adversary has spent time beyond a mere cut and paste approach to an answer; it is a clue to how sophisticated the defendant is, and what kind of fight he will put up. On the other hand if an attorney explains a potential defense too much, it may eliminate the surprise, and give a plaintiff's counsel the opportunity to counsel his client before the deposition or trial. In addition, too much detail can paint the client in a corner.

B. A Written Contract Waiving Any Claim of Ownership

Since the essential purpose of a constructive trust is to prevent unjust enrichment,[5] a perfect defense would be there could not have been unjust enrichment. One

---

3. *See* Bruno v. Sant'Elia, 52 A.D.3d 556 (N.Y. App. Div. 2008); Glenesk v Guidance Realty Corp., 36 A.D.2d 852, 853 (N.Y. App. Div. 1971); Bentivegna v. Meenan Oil Co., 126 A.D.2d 506, 508 (N.Y. App. Div. 1987).

4. Cal. Code Civ. Proc., § 431.30(b)(2).

5. Coco v. Coco, 107 A.D.2d 21, 24 (N.Y. App. Div. 1985).

method of proving that there is no unjust enrichment is if the alleged trustee originally purchased the property from the alleged beneficiary pursuant to a written contract. Written contracts for real estate normally indicate that the transfer is permanent and irrevocable, with no ifs, ands, or buts. In many jurisdictions, the existence of an express, enforceable contract bars recovery under quasi-contractual theories, such as unjust enrichment, for events arising out of the same subject matter.[6]

Therefore, if a defendant is in the rare situation of having entered into a valid written contract concerning the subject of the constructive trust, he may be freed of any claim that the alleged beneficiary had a right to the return of the property. This is because "[t]he theory of unjust enrichment lies as a quasi-contract claim. It is an obligation law creates in the absence of any agreement."[7]

In New York, the law currently seems to be that this kind of written contract would bar a party to the contract at issue from even claiming a constructive trust case.[8] Other states seem to have similar law.[9] Other cases do not necessarily agree. The D.C. Court of Appeals held that constructive trusts may be issued in contravention of written contracts, such as deeds to real property, where there

6. *See* Fortune Prod. Co. v. Conoco, Inc., 52 S.W.3d 671, 684 (Tex. 2000); Clark-Fitzpatrick, Inc. v. Long Is. R.R. Co., 70 N.Y.2d 382, 388 (1987); California Med. Assn. v. Aetna U.S. Healthcare of California, Inc., 94 Cal. App. 4th 151, 172 (Cal. Ct. App. 2001).

7. Goldman v. Metro Life Ins. Co., 5 N.Y.3d 561, 572 (2005).

8. *See In re* First Central Fin. Corp., 377 F.3d 209, 213–16 (2d Cir. 2004); Petrello v. White, 412 F. Supp. 2d 215, 232–33 (E.D.N.Y. 2006); Hamrick v. Guralnick, 146 A.D.3d 606 (N.Y. App. Div. 2017).

9. *See* Rankin v. Naftalis, 557 S.W.2d 940, 944 (Tex. 1977); Conquest v. WCM Mortg. Corp., 247 F. Supp. 3d 618, 644 (E.D. Pa. 2017).

is strong evidence of inequitable conduct.[10] A Colorado court held that "[I]f the elements of unjust enrichment are established, a plaintiff may be entitled to relief, even in the face of a contract with a clearly expressed contrary intent, if justice requires."[11]

Even if the argument does not work in the context of avoiding unjust enrichment, it may work to disprove a confidential relationship, in certain contexts. "A relationship that is characterized by an arms-length contract, which was negotiated by attorneys, is not the stuff of fiduciary relationships."[12]

Deciding whether written and signed papers explicitly indicating an agreement to permanently give up property, would prohibit a party from claiming a constructive trust case, is like deciding what happens when an unstoppable force meets an unmoving object. On the one hand, the law is generally set up so that when people sign contracts, the courts will generally enforce them, on the presumption that people are rational, and have the right to decide their own fates in a manner that absolutely resolves their rights. Presumably, with enough concrete, specific language, there must be a way for people to purchase or sell property in a manner that makes them absolutely sure that the transaction is final, without any takebacks. On the other hand, the entire concept of a constructive trust is that sometimes people who have a close relationship to others will find a way to obtain

10. Gray v. Gray, 412 A.2d 1208, 1210–11 (D.C. 1980).

11. Martinez v. Colo. Dep't of Human Servs., 97 P.3d 152, 159 (Colo. App. 2003).

12. Briggs v. Good Year Tire & Rubber Co., 79 F. Supp. 2d 228, 238 (W.D.N.Y. 1999).

property from another, and if the transaction is generally unfair, then a trustee should not be given a magic formula that would insulate him. What is really fair here is not so clear.

But if the case for a constructive trust is extreme enough, a plaintiff might choose to focus not so much on the unjust enrichment aspect of it but instead on the contract itself. One might consider arguing that the contract should be vacated. This is because the rule indicating that valid contracts defeat a constructive trust case only apply (obviously) if the contract is valid. If one can claim a basis to invalidate the contract, then one can try to claim a constructive trust. Some examples include duress, undue influence, or lack of mental capacity. For example, in *Kinsel v. Lindsey*, the Texas Supreme Court affirmed a court's decision to grant constructive trust relief after the jury determined both (1) that the grantors lacked mental capacity to execute the contracts, and (2) that they were unduly influenced into doing so.[13]

C. Statute of Limitations and Laches

For a constructive trust, the states have no consistent statute of limitations rules. New York has one of the simpler ones, because a "constructive trust" is considered a cause of action and not necessarily a form of relief. In New York, the statute of limitations is six years.[14] But in many other states, the court examines the underlying cause of action, such as whether one is seeking relief due to fraud.

13. 526 S.W.3d 411, 418, 425–27 (Tex. 2017).
14. N.Y. CPLR 213(1).

In certain cases it becomes unclear. For example, an action for the recovery of real property within the meaning of California's relevant statute has a five-year limitations period.[15] But in some circumstances, the three-year statute of limitations for fraud would apply.[16]

Once the length of the statute of limitations is resolved, the court must also determine when the clock had started ticking. It is easy enough to say that it applies "upon the occurrence of the wrongful act giving rise to a duty of restitution,"[17] but applying that becomes more complicated. One court indicated that a limitations period does not run between a trustee and his beneficiary until there has been a repudiation of the constructive trust.[18] Another held that in the context of a resulting trust, the statute of limitations does not run on a beneficiary "until he has actual knowledge of repudiation or breach of trust."[19]

One must also consider whether the state's law distinguishes between a statute of limitations for a resulting trust and a constructive trust. In at least one state, "Some courts have held that the statute of limitations does not apply to resulting trusts, since the enforcement of a resulting trust in equity is governed by the doctrine of laches and not by the statute of limitations."[20]

---

15. Cal. Code Civ. Proc. § 318.
16. *Id.* § 338.
17. Sitkowski v. Petzing, 175 A.D.2d 801, 802 (N.Y. App. Div. 1991).
18. Miller v. Miller, 83 N.M. 230, 490 P.2d 672 (1971).
19. Martin v. Kehl, 145 Cal. App. 3d 228, 237 (1983).
20. Key v. Trattmann, 959 So. 2d 339, 342 n.1 (Fla. Dist. Ct. App. 2007) (citations and internal quotation marks omitted).

In some states, where generally a cause of action does not arise until a demand and refusal, and it is within the plaintiff's power to make such a demand, the statute will commence to run after the lapse of a reasonable time.[21] The nature of the agreement and the circumstances surrounding it will determine what qualifies as a "reasonable time."

In New York, the general law indicates that there are two ways of looking at when the statute of limitations begins to run. If the constructive trustee "acquired the property wrongfully" then the wrongful act is when he "acquired" it.[22] That is presumably because in most cases the property would be deemed to be "held adversely from the date of acquisition."

The other measurement comes into play when the "constructive trustee wrongfully withholds property acquired lawfully from the beneficiary, in which case the property would be held adversely from the date the trustee breaches or repudiates the agreement to transfer the property."[23] One court put it this way: "The statute of limitations for a constructive trust claim starts to run upon the occurrence of the wrongful act giving rise to a duty of restitution. . . . In general, the date of the 'wrongful act' is the date that the party holding legal title takes some action that is inconsistent with the promise he made to the transferor."[24]

---

21. *See* Southward v. Foy, 65 Nev. 694, 705–06 (1948).

22. Sitkowski v. Petzing, 175 A.D.2d 801, 802 (N.Y. App. Div. 1991).

23. *Id.*

24. Jaffer v. Hirji, No. 14 Civ. 2127 (KMK), 2017 WL 1169665, at *8 (S.D.N.Y. Mar. 28, 2017) (internal quotation marks and citations omitted); *partially reversed on other grounds,* 887 F.3d 111 (2d Cir. 2018).

A breach or repudiation of an agreement would include informing the beneficiary that the trustee would never transfer the property to him.[25] It could also apply if a party encumbers property with a mortgage without the beneficiary's consent.[26]

Some situations are not so clear. For example, what if the constructive trustee acquired the property "wrongfully," but then kept promising, for a period beyond the statute of limitations, to deed it to the beneficiary? And then what if he finally did not do so? It might be difficult to determine when the time limit starts ticking. In any event, a good attorney representing a beneficiary would protect his client as much as possible, and indicate that the wrongful act must have taken place within the statutory deadline, or that tolling applied.

At least one case went beyond the traditional method of determining when the statute of limitations is measured from. In that case, one brother purchased property supposedly on behalf of both brothers. As indicated earlier, the traditional rules measure the statute of limitation either from when the property was obtained in a "wrongful" manner or from the date constructive trustee wrongfully withholds property acquired lawfully from the beneficiary. Neither of those would seem to apply in that kind of case though. The court simply remanded the matter, so the court could resolve when the purchasing brother "allegedly breached any agreement by

---

25. *See* Held v. Kaufman, 91 N.Y.2d 425 (1998).

26. *See* Loeuis v. Grushin, 126 A.D.3d 761 (N.Y. App. Div. 2015).

refusing to convey . . . interest in the property [to his non-purchasing brother]."[27]

Other cases apply these rules loosely, in favor of a plaintiff. For example, in *Dombek v. Reiman*, the plaintiff allowed certain people to use money from joint accounts to purchase real estate in 1994, and allegedly defendants agreed to let him live in the premises rent free.[28] Defendants changed their mind and evicted him in 2001. When the plaintiff filed the case the same year, the court did not apply the 1994 date, and held the case was timely filed. The issue becomes confusing because the real estate itself was purchased lawfully, and the premises were not technically obtained from the beneficiary himself. If courts were operated by robots and not judges, one might assume the 1994 date would be appropriate as the date from which the statute of limitation should be measured. But the court used the latter date.

Perhaps a better rule, or definition, of when the statute of limitations begins to run was used in *Mardiros v. Ghaly*.[29] In that case, the court held that the statute of limitations begins to run either "(1) when the constructive trustee's interest in the property first becomes adverse to the plaintiff's interests, or (2) when the constructive trustee wrongfully withholds property acquired lawfully from the beneficiary." That's the better definition for a plaintiff, but the case is a bit old. In any event, a plaintiff in a bind on timing will likely want to cite that kind of language.

---

27. Maric Piping, Inc. v. Maric, 271 A.D.2d 507 (N.Y. App. Div. 2000).

28. 298 A.D.2d 876 (N.Y. App. Div. 2002).

29. 206 A.D.2d 414 (N.Y. App. Div. 1994).

Even if the deadline from the statute of limitations might be deemed to have passed, not all hope is lost for a potential plaintiff. There are certain exceptions to the statute of limitations, but one must "aver evidentiary facts establishing that the case falls within an exception to the Statute of Limitations."[30] One kind of exception would be tolling. What kind of excuse the courts might accept for a constructive trust case is vague.

There is a potential of claiming that the equities of a situation prevent the trustee from raising the statute of limitations defense. This can arise "where it is the defendant's affirmative wrongdoing which produced the long delay between the accrual of the cause of action and the institution of the legal proceeding."[31] However, if a plaintiff seeks to make that claim, the attorney should make sure to raise facts within the complaint alleging conduct to which the doctrine would be applicable. Otherwise, the plaintiff may not raise it in opposition to a potential summary judgment motion to dismiss the case.[32]

There is a serious potential problem if an attorney uses the phrase "statute of limitations," in the answer to a complaint, by itself, without further explanation. A careful attorney who has a serious potential defense on this ground will avoid just writing those three words and then patting himself on the back. Instead, he should reveal detail about when the statute of limitations could have conceivably begun to run, and perhaps even further indicate how many years have elapsed from that date. That

---

30. Savarese v. Shatz, 273 A.D.2d 219 (N.Y. App. Div. 2000).

31. Zumpano v. Quinn, 6 NY3d 666, 673 (2006) (internal quotation marks and ellipses omitted).

32. *See* Florio v. Cook, 48 N.Y.2d 792 (N.Y. 1979).

kind of information may not be necessary, because the high court in New York held that a bare assertion of a statute of limitations defense in an answer would be sufficient to withstand the pleading particularity requirements of the relevant state statute, CPLR 3013.[33] More recently, a New York appellate court suggested that it was time for its high court to revisit the issue.[34] In any event, it is best to avoid making the statute of limitations defense vague.

Other cases make the law more confusing. For example, in Florida, one court held that it would not make sense to use the preceding timing issues about statute of limitations at all for a constructive trust case, or at least in certain cases. It indicated that the right to relief is immediate because "[a] constructive trust has its inception in an antagonistic relationship. It is founded in a situation produced by fraud, undue influence, abuse of confidence or mistake."[35] The same court held that "[t]he rights of the beneficiary as against the antagonistic claims of the trustee under a deed such as the one before us come into being when the deed is recorded or at the earliest when the beneficiary knew or should have known of the adverse claim of the trustee."[36] This seems odd because at least in many cases, there is no known abuse of confidence until the promise to return the property is breached. Later case law in Florida possibly

---

33. Immediate v. St. John Queens Hosp.., 48 N.Y.2d 671, 673 (1979).

34. Scholastic Inc. v. Pace Plumbing Corp., 129 A.D.3d 75, 81 (N.Y. App. Div. 2015).

35. Wadlington v. Edwards, 92 So. 2d 629, 632 (Fla. 1957).

36. *Id.*

indicates a change of heart, and that applying repudiation of a constructive trust as the starting point for the statute of limitations is just fine.[37]

If the issue concerns real property, there may be a special law that applies. For example, Florida Statute section 95.231(2) provides that "[a]fter 20 years from the recording of a deed or the probate of a will purporting to convey real property, no person shall assert any claim to the property against the claimants under the deed or will or their successors in title." Depending on whether the court interprets such a statute literally, or whether it interprets it loosely as in "twenty years from the date in which the agreement to reconvey was repudiated," could make a major difference.

The ugly stepsister of a statute of limitations defense is "laches." This is a common phrase that attorneys like to include in a laundry list of affirmative defenses. That word alone in an answer does very little. As one court noted, an affirmative defense stating merely that "[p]laintiff's claims are barred by the equitable doctrine of laches" was correctly dismissed "as pleading only a bare legal conclusion without supporting facts."[38]

For the laches claim to win the day, there must have been not only an unreasonable and inexcusable delay, but it would also need to result in either acquiescence in the act that is the subject of the complaint, or prejudice

37. Collinson v. Miller, 903 So. 2d 221, 227–30 (Fla. Dist. Ct. App. 2005).

38. Comm'rs of the State Ins. Fund v. Ramos, 63 A.D.3d 453, 453 (N.Y. App. Div. 2009).

to the defendant from the delay.[39] To put it another way, one must prove two elements: "(1) unreasonable delay by one having legal or equitable rights in asserting them; and (2) a good faith change of position by another to his detriment because of the delay."[40]

Acquiescence in the context of a constructive trust may be a non sequitur. It may not fit at all, because many constructive trusts are premised on first providing property to a defendant, and then expecting its return. Alternatively, proving "prejudice" may be difficult. It could be proved by "a showing of injury, change of position, loss of evidence, or some other disadvantage resulting from the delay."[41] Perhaps, for example, an alleged trustee could explain briefly in such a defense that certain witnesses who could have testified in his defense, have died. A mere claim that there may be faded memory will not work, normally, because that is one of the policy reasons behind the statute of limitations.[42] Another possibility might be to explain that the alleged trustee has already spent time and effort renovating the premises, and lost the opportunity to spend funds to purchase other real property, due to the unreasonable delay in the plaintiff's decision to file suit. These kinds of arguments, even if brief, should go into the pleading.

---

39. *See* Markell v. Markell, 91 A.D.3d 832, 834 (N.Y. App. Div. 2012); Miller v. Eisenhower Med. Ctr., 27 Cal. 3d 614, 624 (1980).

40. Rogers v. Ricane Enter., Inc., 772 S.W.2d 76, 80 (Tex. 1989).

41. Skrodelis v. Norbergs, 272 A.D.2d 316, 317 (N.Y. App. Div. 2000).

42. See Wakefield v. Bevly, 704 S.W.2d 339, 345 (Tex. App.–Corpus Christi 1985, no writ).

D. Innocent Beneficiary versus Good Faith Purchaser

No matter what evidence there is that a plaintiff would have at one point been entitled to constructive trust relief, if the asset has been transferred for value, it becomes free and clear. Therefore, one nice way around a constructive trust case is to prove that your client is a bona fide purchaser of the asset in question. A bona fide purchaser takes free of a constructive trust.[43]

The rule may seem odd, because the general rule is that "a thief cannot convey a good title to stolen property."[44] However, there are exceptions to that rule, including when money has been put into circulation and has come to the hands of bona fide holders. In that kind of case, the right of the owner to reclaim it ends. And in the case of a constructive trust, once a bona fide purchaser takes ownership, the claim to that particular property ends. Perhaps that is also because a trustee does not technically take property by "theft" normally.

A bona fide purchaser is one "who takes property (1) for valuable consideration, (2) in good faith, and (3) absent notice of any adverse claims."[45] There is no basis for a constructive trust against this kind of person, because he is not guilty of unjust enrichment if he is

---

43. *See, e.g.*, Pluemer v. Pluemer, 322 Wis.2d 138, 151 (Wis. Ct. App. 2009); *In re* Marriage of Allen, 724 P.2d 651, 658 (Colo. 1986); Hunnicutt Constr., Inc. v. Stewart Title, 187 Ariz. 301, 305–06 (Ariz. Ct. App. 1996).

44. Newton v. Porter, 69 N.Y. 133, 137 (1877).

45. Groza-Vance v. Vance, 162 Ohio App. 3d 510, 526 (Ohio Ct. App. 2005) (citation omitted).

permitted to keep it.[46] As one court noted, "Where a person holding property transfers it to another in violation of his duty to a third person, the third person can reach the property in the hands of the transferee by means of a constructive trust unless the transferee is a bona fide purchaser."[47] In one case addressing this issue, the court indicated that a bona fide purchaser can even include one who pays off the transferor's mortgage, a note, or any debt. But if the buyer has any knowledge, even enough to put him on inquiry that there may be an outstanding right in conflict with the title he is about to acquire, he cannot be considered to be a bona fide purchaser.[48]

On a related topic, a judgment creditor, such as one that obtained a judgment or even levies an execution upon the property, is not a bona fide purchaser. This is regardless of the creditor's ignorance of the constructive trust claim.[49]

If an alleged gratuitous donee has the property at issue, a plaintiff should attempt to conduct discovery against anyone in the chain of title, including to find out what consideration was paid. In theory, a plaintiff might need to retain an expert to prove the actual value of the asset at the time of the purchase, in comparison to the sum provided. During depositions, a bona fide purchaser should also be questioned about what he or she

---

46. *See* Ga. Malone & Co. v. Rieder, 19 N.Y.3d 511, 517 (N.Y. 2012).

47. Richards v. Richards, 58 Wis. 2d 290, 298 (Wis. 1973) (citation and internal brackets omitted).

48. Giordano v. Giordano, 991 N.E.2d 189 (Mass. App. Ct. 2013).

49. *See* Hunnicutt Constr. v. Stewart Title Trust, 187 Ariz. 301, 305 (Ariz. Ct. App. 1996) (citations omitted).

had found out about the property prior to the purchase, and attempt to elicit information about whether the entire transaction would have made a reasonable person believe they were getting something for nothing.

If the defendant, on the other hand, received the property without valuable consideration, such as through inheritance, then the constructive trust claim can still be effective. Constructive trusts have been imposed in cases where the person against whom the constructive trust was imposed was an innocent beneficiary and had engaged in no wrongdoing.[50] One example is *Bohannon v. Trotman*,[51] in which the court held that property in the hands of the beneficiaries of a will is subject to a constructive trust in favor of a plaintiff if a testator was wrongfully induced to exclude plaintiff from any participation in his estate, even if the beneficiaries were not parties to the wrongful act.

Another example involves insurance proceeds. For instance, in one case, an ex-husband had an obligation under a divorce judgment to include his minor children as life insurance beneficiaries. He improperly changed the beneficiary to his current wife. The court held she would be subject to a constructive trust action. As the court put it, "the mere ignorance of the recipient of the original impropriety did not make the recipient . . . a bona fide purchaser."[52]

---

50. *See* Connecticut Gen. Life Ins. v. Merkel, 90 Wis.2d 126, 131 (Wis. Ct. App. 1979); Dyll v. Adams, 167 F.3d 945, 948 (5th Cir. 1999).

51. 214 N.C. 706 (N.C. 1939).

52. Richards v. Richards, 58 Wis.2d 290, 298 (Wis. 1973).

E. Unclean Hands

Since a constructive trust is an equitable cause of action, it comes with some handicaps, not involved in a cause of action for pure monetary damages. One is to ensure that the party seeking relief was not guilty of immoral or unconscionable conduct, that is, "unclean hands," when the constructive trust was established. If the court were to enforce a constructive trust in those kinds of circumstances, it could be taken as an open invitation that people are free to set up constructive trusts for immoral purposes, and then force the court to act as an enabler, like Carmella Soprano. If the party setting up the constructive trust has dirty hands, then asking the court to enforce it will dirty the court's hands too.

Courts have at least two goals. One is to provide protection to those who were harmed. The other is to protect their own integrity. Sometimes they cannot do both, and a court can have difficulty deciding which side to take. If the court rules that a plaintiff has been seriously taken advantage of by the supposed trustee, but the plaintiff has slightly dirty hands, should he be left without form of relief? If that were the case, the primary issues in the case could change—not from whether there was a true constructive trust and what relief would otherwise be appropriate, but instead a focus on how clean the plaintiff's hands were. And since it's rare for a human being to be perfectly innocent, especially in a constructive trust case, to apply this principle fully might deprive a great number of people from relief. On the other hand, the court cannot approve of allowing people to set up constructive trusts as a way of committing inequitable acts. "The court does not want to touch an unlawful transaction with a ten-foot pole."[53]

The issue is so delicate and nuanced, that the law sometimes becomes inconsistent, not only within the United States as a whole but sometimes within a state itself. Therefore a practitioner can sometimes find helpful law on his side, no matter what the side.

Some cases indicate that the unclean hands doctrine "is never used unless the plaintiff is guilty of immoral, unconscionable conduct and even then only when the conduct relied on is directly related to the subject matter of the litigation and the party seeking to invoke the doctrine was injured by such conduct."[54] But not all cases indicate there must be injury to the party seeking to invoke the doctrine. For example, the U.S. Supreme Court indicated that a party is remediless in a court of equity if his conduct is "offensive to the dictates of natural justice."[55]

One example of this potentially "offensive" behavior was described in a Virginia federal case. A party had been fired for misconduct, and then misled defendants about those reasons. The defendants then believed he was worthy of being trusted, and entered into a fiduciary relationship with him. When the defendants allegedly

53. *In re* Flanagan, 373 B.R. 216, 224 (Bankr. D. Conn. 2007).

54. National Distillers Chemical Corp. v. Seyopp Corp., 17 N.Y.2d 12, 15–16 (1966) (internal citation and quotation marks omitted). *See also* Willis v. Donnelly, 118 S.W.3d 10, 38 (Tex. App. 2003) *aff'd in part and rev'd in part on other grounds*, 199 S.W.3d 266 (Tex. 2006); Mascenic v. Anderson, 53 Ill. App. 3d 971, 972 (Ill. App. Ct. 1977).

55. Keystone Driller Co. v. Gen. Excavator Co., 290 U.S. 240, 245 (1933).

violated that relationship and took advantage of a business opportunity, the plaintiff sought constructive trust relief. The court held that since defendants would never have entered into a fiduciary relationship with him if they knew the truth, the plaintiff could not seek constructive trust relief.[56]

Case law indicates that a common form of unclean hands in a constructive trust case is when the plaintiff transferred property to another to avoid losing it to actual or potential creditors. Plaintiffs know that once they officially do not own property, the chance of losing that property to a creditor is seriously reduced.

Should the law officially recognize this method, and rule in favor of an actual or potential debtor who had feared having to pay out sums he legitimately owed, and used the constructive trust device as a means to hide away his funds?

Courts have come to various conclusions about how to handle this situation. There are many potential issues at stake. One issue is whether that kind of behavior is immoral or unconscionable to begin with. Some cases have implicitly indicated that this depends on whether the creditors were "actual" or just "potential." As just one example, most people would not call it immoral for a person who looks at life in a big picture way and wants to protect his assets by giving them to loved ones, to ensure they would never be lost to any potential creditor. It's a very different thing when the same person knows he is

56. Bocek v. JGA Assocs., LLC, 1:11-cv-0546 (JCC/JFA), at *17–18 (E.D. Va. Mar. 23, 2016).

about to be sued, or is already being sued, to hide away those assets from a particular creditor by giving them to relatives. Statutes indicate that those kinds of transactions are inherently fraudulent.[57]

Many cases address these issues. For example, in *Tordai v. Tordai*,[58] a man who transferred property to his wife in order to shelter it from "potential business creditors" was still entitled to constructive trust relief. This may have been in part because there is a difference between a "potential" creditor and an "actual" one, but this is a difficult distinction to make. In another case, in which a man wished to purchase real property and, then in order to hide it from his wife, "gave" it to his girlfriend, the court held that this is not a form of unclean hands. It allowed the man to pursue his constructive trust case. The court held that the "immoral conduct" was directed at his wife, and did not directly injure his girlfriend.[59] And in yet another way of resolving the issue, at least one court held that only a creditor can raise the unclean hands defense to a constructive trust case.[60] The concept behind such cases may be in part based on the fact that states have specific statutes that are designed to prevent debtors from transferring property for no consideration. But those statutes only permit the creditor to obtain relief.

57. *See, e.g.*, N.Y. Debtor and Creditor Law.

58. 109 A.D.2d 996, 997–98 (N.Y. App. Div. 1985).

59. Columbo v. Columbo, 50 A.D.3d 617, 619 (N.Y. App. Div. 2008).

60. Cornwell v. Cornwell, 116 N.H. 205, 210 (N.H. 1976).

Another method of resolving this issue is the "no harm, no foul" rule. That is, if no actual harm has come to the potential creditors, the trial court can deny the application of the unclean hands doctrine.[61] Surprisingly, even if the issue is a government-related issue, such as a tax lien, at least one court held that so long as the tax lien was ultimately released, the grantors could still recover their property that they transferred to avoid that lien.[62]

There is another set of other decisions (some even within the same state), which is that so long as the party who transferred property away did so in an effort to prevent creditors from reaching it, he cannot use the constructive trust theory to get his property back. The seminal New York Court of Appeals case concerning unclean hands in a constructive trust case is *Pattison v. Pattison*.[63] In that case, the plaintiff's nephew had a judgment against him. To keep his property out of reach of the nephew, he transferred it to his sister, with the alleged understanding that she would have to give it back someday, after the judgment was paid. Eventually, he paid the nephew, and then demanded that his sister return the property. When she did not, he sued her. But the court did not allow this kind of game; the plaintiff's case was dismissed. Other New York cases also appear to indicate that it is irrelevant whether creditors or potential creditors were injured; the mere fact that the plaintiff wanted

61. *See, e.g.*, Nelson v. Emmert, 105 S.W.3d 563, 568–69 (Mo. Ct. App. 2003); Estate of Blanco, 86 Cal. App. 3d 826 (Cal. Ct. App.1978).

62. Webb v. Manifold Bus. Investments, Inc., 261 Or. 276 (1972).

63. 301 N.Y. 65 (1950).

to prevent them from enforcing rights is enough to bar him from relief in a constructive trust case.[64]

New York seems to have a split personality on this issue; some cases follow one view about creditors actually being affected, as indicated earlier in this chapter, and some indicate that this is irrelevant. Whichever argument is in one's favor, a New York attorney can find the right set of cases. There may be no Rosetta Stone which explains the divergence.

Michigan has followed the tough standard against plaintiffs rule, dismissing a constructive trust case in which the plaintiff was trying to defraud creditors by parking his assets with another, and thus sheltering his property. The court did not examine whether the creditors were actually defrauded, and simply held that the plaintiff was not in a position to complain because he should have known that "there is, as the old aphorism puts it, no honor among thieves."[65]

If an attorney is representing the defendant, he may have to do a diligent search for cases in his own state that stand for this proposition. If that does not work, at least one can always argue that the particular case calls for applying the unclean hands doctrine. Application of the doctrine turns upon the facts of each particular case

64. Farino v. Farino, 88 A.D.2d 902, 902–03 (N.Y. App. Div. 1982); Dolny v. Borck, 61 A.D.3d 817 (N.Y. App. Div. 2009) Festinger v. Edrich, 32 A.D.3d 412, 414 (N.Y. App. Div. 2006); Wong v. Wong, 293 A.D.2d 387, 387 (N.Y. App. Div. 2002); Flores v. Guambana, 162 A.D.3d 983 (N.Y. App. Div. 2018).

65. Matouk v. Robert L. Barrick Tr., No. 328983, at *10 (Mich. Ct. App. May 2, 2017).

and is therefore "left to the sound discretion of the fact finder."[66]

The ultimate kind of unclean hands is when a plaintiff has transferred away property, in order to avoid debts to creditors, and even goes so far as to file a bankruptcy proceeding without listing himself as the owner of the property. If the bankruptcy court discharges the plaintiff's debts, but the plaintiff later seeks to claim that the property still belongs to him under a constructive trust theory, his case should be dismissed.[67] This is not technically based on an "unclean hands" argument, but is instead based on judicial estoppel. That means a party may not take a position in an earlier case, obtain results in his favor, and then change positions simply because his interests have changed.

Another potential "unclean hands" argument concerns fraud upon a lender of the property itself. In one case, the parties had defrauded a mortgage company by adding a third party to the contract of sale, the mortgage application, and the deed, in order to obtain a mortgage when purchasing a house. The plaintiff sought a partition and defendant sought a constructive trust against the plaintiff's interest in the house. Both claims were dismissed. "Because both parties had unclean hands in connection with the purchase of this house, they are both barred from all equitable relief."[68] In another case, the plaintiff set up a short sale, and arranged for his nephew

---

66. Wiglesworth v. Taylor, 239 Va. 603, 608 (1990).
67. *See, e.g.*, Bihn v. Connelly, 162 A.D.3d 626 (N.Y. App. Div. 2018).
68. Vasquez v. Zambrano, 196 A.D.2d 840 (N.Y. App. Div. 1993).

to purchase the property, with the secret intention that the nephew would eventually transfer it back to the uncle. In part because this was a fraud on the bank, and that the uncle was secretly trying to regain title to the property for significantly less than what he owed the bank, using subterfuge, the constructive trust relief was denied.[69] However, some cases rule in favor of constructive trusts when title to property was taken in the name of a family member in order to qualify for a mortgage upon showing a promise to reconvey.[70]

For this defense, does it matter if the defendant knew (at the time of the transaction) that the plaintiff was attempting to commit any kind of fraud? In one case, the plaintiff admitted he transferred property to defendants in order to put it out of reach of creditors. The court dismissed the constructive trust due to unclean hands, and held specifically that the question of whether the defendants "knew of the fraudulent purpose of the transaction is irrelevant."[71]

It is crucial for an attorney to know how to use this defense effectively. In many cases in which the plaintiff originally owned the premises at issue, he has transferred it to the defendant for a reason. For example, the plaintiff may have done so because he tried to prevent someone else from obtaining his assets, or tried to save it somehow through a straw buyer. In either case, the more

69. Hajji v. Esho, No. 329737, at *4 (Mich. Ct. App. Mar. 23, 2017).

70. *See* Vincent v. Vincent, 80 A.D.2d 582 (N.Y. App. Div. 1981); Djamoos v. Djamoos, 153 A.D.2d 871 (N.Y. App. Div. 1989).

71. Dolny v. Borck, 61 A.D.3d 817 (N.Y. App. Div. 2009).

the plaintiff can be convinced to admit these things in a deposition, the more likely he will be deemed to have unclean hands, and without a right to seek equitable relief like a constructive trust.

Despite certain language in some cases indicating that even a speck of dirt on the plaintiff knocks out a constructive trust case, courts will also look at the underlying circumstances. For example, in a California Supreme Court case in which a young daughter convinced her aged father to transfer assets to herself, partly in order to hide his assets from the father's second wife, the court denied the "unclean hands" defense, holding that "though a deed made for an improper purpose is unfairly procured through the undue influence of the grantee, in violation of a fiduciary relationship, abuse of confidence, oppression or fraud, a court of equity will still grant relief to one in fault. Such relief will not be denied to a party least in fault against one who has led him into the act by a violation of confidence. They are not in equal wrong."[72] In one Michigan case, the court held that one party with unclean hands may not avoid the application of the doctrine by arguing that the other party also has unclean hands.[73] On the other hand, the U.S. Supreme Court has held that no matter how improper the behavior of the defendant, the court cannot grant equitable relief if the plaintiff is guilty of unclean hands.[74]

---

72. Birney v. Birney, 217 Cal. 353, 359 (1933).

73. City of Fraser v. Almeda Univ., 314 Mich. App 79, 100 (Mich. Ct. App. 2016).

74. Precision Instrument Mfg. Co. v. Auto. Maint. Mach. Co. 324 U.S. 806, 814–15 (1945).

Despite the preceding rules, the court always has to protect one of its own—that is, the government itself. Therefore, if one can prove that the original transfer was to avoid a government penalty such as seizure, excise taxes, forfeitures, or fines, or to obtain an unwarranted governmental benefit such as eligibility for Medicaid, it's highly unlikely the government (through the court) will give that a stamp of approval. For example, in *Bruner v. Bruner*, the court held that the clean hands doctrine barred a resulting or constructive trust on property that plaintiff induced his parents to purchase with his funds so that he could "avoid[ ] certain taxes and obtain[ ] other advantages."[75] On the other hand (there is always another hand), as indicated earlier, at least one case held that if a transaction was conducted in order to avoid a tax lien, then so long as the tax lien was ultimately paid off, that will not bar constructive trust relief.

One more critical issue is—who has the dirtier hands, or whether there are equally dirty hands. Some cases indicate that if the parties have equally dirty hands (which is known by the fancy Latin term *in pari delicto*), then the court will leave things the way they are, and not issue a constructive trust.[76]

---

75. 338 F.3d 1172 (10th Cir. 2003); *see also* Hardy v. Hardy, 910 N.E.2d 851, 853 (Ind. Ct. App. 2009); McMichael v. Flynn, 686 So.2d 254, 256 (Ala. Civ. App. 1995); Hood v. Hood, 46 N.C. App. 298, 300, (N.C. Ct. App. 1980); Shattuck v. Peck, 70 A.3d 922, 926 (Vt. 2013).

76. *See, e.g., In re* Flanagan, 373 B.R. 216, 229 (Bankr. D. Conn. 2007).

F. Whether Monetary Damages Suffice

"What's the answer to 99 out of 100 questions? Money."

—Cameron Crowe, *Vanilla Sky*

State law is not consistent when it comes to whether a plaintiff seeking a constructive trust must also prove that money damages would not be sufficient. In most cases, the plaintiff will have a leg up if the underlying res is some sort of property other than a fund of money. If the res is unique, so much the better.[77] Best of all is real property, especially if your client intends to live in the space. But even if there is just a specific fund of money, a plaintiff can still potentially obtain a constructive trust.

Some courts, like those in New York, consistently hold that a plaintiff must prove that money damages would not be adequate compensation.[78] If, for example, the plaintiff does not claim that defendant would be unable to repay sums the plaintiff contributed, then there may not be a constructive trust case. And if the New York court believes that the primary relief the plaintiff is seeking is a money judgment, then the equitable relief will also be barred.[79] Other states have the same attitude: that equitable remedies are not available if there is an adequate

77. *See* Locken v. Locken, 98 Nev. 369, 372 (Nev. 1982).

78. *See* Evans v. Winston & Strawn, 303 A.D.2d 331, 333 (N.Y. App. Div. 2003); Knopf v. Sanford, 123 A.D.3d 521, 522 (N.Y. App. Div. 2014).

79. *See* Credit Agricole Indosuez v. Rossiyskiy Kredit Bank 94 NY2d 541, 548 (N.Y. 2000).

remedy at law, especially in the context of a constructive trust.[80]

In South Dakota, for example, it can be especially deadly to a plaintiff if he claims money damages in the alternative to a constructive trust, and provides no reason why money damages would be inadequate.[81] Oregon is similarly tough, indicating one cannot obtain a constructive trust if the remedy is identical to a potential legal remedy. This rule exists "not because of any supposed primacy of legal over equitable remedies, but because constructive trust is superfluous."[82] As another court put it, "An examination of the record in this case reveals that [the plaintiff] is not entitled to the equitable remedy of a constructive trust because it has an adequate remedy at law."[83]

Other courts are more lenient. For example, one Missouri court cited a treatise, and held that in a suit to establish a constructive trust, the plaintiff is not required to prove the inadequacy of the remedy at law and is "able to elect freely between the relief which the law can give him and the constructive trust remedy."[84] Californians are similarly relaxed with this issue. "In California, as

80. *See* Nelson v. Nelson, 288 Kan. 570, 597 (Kan. 2009) (citation omitted); Joel v. Joel, 2009 CA 474, 430 n.10 (Miss. 2010).

81. Carolina Park Assoc., LLC v. Marino, 400 S.C. 1, 8 (S.C. 2012).

82. Evergreen West Bus. Ctr., LLC v. Emmert, 323 P.3d 250, 258–59 (Or. 2014) citing 1 Restatement (Third) of Restitution and Unjust Enrichment § 4 cmt. e (2011).

83. Mitsubishi Int'l. v. Cardinal Textile Sales, 14 F.3d 1507, 1519 (11th Cir. 1994).

84. Taylor-McDonald v. Taylor, 245 S.W.3d 867, 874 (Mo. Ct. App. 2008) (citation omitted).

in most jurisdictions, an action in equity to establish a constructive trust does not depend on the absence of an adequate legal remedy."[85] Mississippi follows this general standard as well.[86]

The good news for a plaintiff is that even if one appears in a state in which the courts need an explanation about why money damages would be insufficient, there are a number of solid reasons. One would be if the defendant is not solvent. (This also gives a plaintiff a right, in the context of a constructive trust, to ask searching questions in discovery about the defendant's financial situation.) But even if the defendant is solvent, a constructive trust may be preferable in certain situations such as "when the property in question has special value for the claimant; when it has appreciated in value; when its value might be difficult to establish; or when recovery of a specific thing is merely less costly than proof and recovery of its value."[87]

Some courts indicate that there could be relatively easy standards to show that money damages would not suffice. "A claimant who seeks restitution via constructive trust—either because property in the hands of the defendant has increased in value, or for the sake of priority against the defendant's general creditors—does not

85. Heckmann v. Ahmanson, 168 Cal. App. 3d 119, 134–33 (Cal. Ct. App. 1985).

86. Wilson v. Scruggs, 371 F. Supp. 2d 837, 841–42 (S.D. Miss 2005).

87. U.S. v. Andrews, 530 F.3d 1232, 1237 (10th Cir. 2008), citing Restatement (Third) of Restitution and Unjust Enrichment § 55(c) (Tentative Draft No. 6, 2008).

usually have to explain to the court why an award of damages does not afford equivalent relief."[88]

Alabama has its own rules. Its high court declared the following: a party has no right to a constructive trust unless (1) "a fiduciary or quasi-fiduciary relation is involved," or (2) "unless relief at law would be inadequate because the chattel is unique or the defendant-wrongdoer is insolvent."[89] South Carolina has its own rules as well. In one case, the court elaborated on how a potential legal remedy must be adequate: "In order to justify a court of equity in refusing to take jurisdiction, the remedy at law must be adequate, and must attain the full end and justice of the case. It is not enough that there is some remedy at law, but that remedy must be as practical, efficient, and prompt as the remedy in equity."[90]

G. Statute of Frauds

In addition to the traditional four Passover questions, an attorney teaching his children about constructive trusts might have them ask, "What makes a constructive trust case different from all other cases concerning real property?" One good answer to that question is "the statute of frauds."

The statute of frauds requires certain contracts to be in a signed writing, in order to be enforceable. Critically,

---

88. 323 P.3d at 257, citing Restatement of the Law (Third), Restitution and Unjust Enrichment § 4 cmt. e (2011).

89. American Family Care, Inc. v. Irwin, 571 So.2d 1053, 1061 (Ala. 1990).

90. Chisolm v. Pryor, 207 S.C. 54, 60 (1945).

a contract that must be in a signed writing is one that concerns the ownership or potential purchase of real property. Since many (if not most) constructive trust cases concern real property, it is critical to understand how the statute of frauds affects constructive trust cases.

The statute of frauds was originally developed centuries ago,[91] in part to prevent plaintiffs from making frivolous claims about matters that would be highly unlikely to be true. A classic example would be a prospective buyer of real property, who claims that a landowner entered an oral contract to sell that property. If one applies the traditional statute of frauds analysis, that potential buyer's claims will be dismissed.

Someone unfamiliar with constructive trusts might presume that the statute of frauds is sufficient to defeat any case in which a party (without a written contract) claims an equitable interest in real property. That assumption is wrong. Although a careful attorney will still raise the statute of frauds in any case it is even conceivably appropriate, the statute of frauds does not preclude "the recognition of a constructive trust affecting an interest in land where a confidential relationship would be abused if there were repudiation, without redress, of a trust orally declared."[92] In an action to impress a constructive trust on real property, the statute of frauds is not a defense because "[s]uch a trust, by its very nature, does not require a writing."[93] California law also indicates that a party is estopped from pleading the statute of frauds

91. Slightly before I was born.

92. Foreman v. Foreman, 251 N.Y. 237, 240 (1929).

93. Vanasco v. Angiolelli, 97 A.D.2d 462, 462 (N.Y. App. Div. 1983).

where necessary to prevent either unconscionable injury or unjust enrichment.[94] Some states even have statutes that explicitly or implicitly indicate that constructive trusts are an exception to the statute of frauds.[95]

The statute of frauds is also a critical reason why courts do not insist that parties prove their rights under express trusts, if they also have a potential constructive trust. As one court put it in a rather poetic way, a constructive trust "is entirely distinct from the express trust in the manner of its creation. Though the same destination may be reached by each, the two roads leading to it are entirely different; one is blocked by the statute of frauds; the other is not."[96]

In short, the court should not apply a statute that was intended to prevent frauds on the court, from being used as a means to help people conduct frauds. Does that mean that if a plaintiff seeks to purchase real property based on an oral contract, he can win the case simply by claiming a constructive trust rather than an oral contract? Would that simple step avoid the death knell of the statute of frauds? It should not be that easy; a careful attorney defending a constructive trust case should try to pigeonhole that kind of action as one that is truly just seeking to enforce an alleged oral contract, or one that is seeking to enforce an alleged oral express trust.

If a potential buyer simply claims that he had an oral contract to purchase real property, and the seller then refused to go through with it, the constructive trust

94. Monarco v. Lo Greco, 35 Cal. 2d 621, 623–24 (1950).

95. *See, e.g.*, NRS 111.205(2). *See also* Tex. Prop. Code § 111.003.

96. Broadway Bldg. Co. v. Salafia, 47 R.I. 263, 265 (1926).

theory will likely not apply at all. In one North Carolina case, the court ruled that a constructive trust kind of case only applies when the defendant *acquired* the property to the plaintiff's detriment. If the defendant owned the property beforehand, for reasons unconnected to a fraud, wrong, or otherwise, and simply refused to sell it, then a constructive trust theory will not work.[97]

What more is necessary to obtain constructive trust relief, beyond simply claiming that the defendant had made an oral agreement to transfer real property to the plaintiff, which the defendant then breached? This is a difficult issue, because we have hundreds of years of case law indicating that oral agreements to sell real property are unenforceable, but we also have at least 100 years of case law indicating that a constructive trust case concerning real property cannot be defeated by a mere statute of frauds argument.

What about a case in which the plaintiff originally owned the property, transferred it to the defendant based on an oral agreement that defendant would transfer it back, and then the defendant failed to do so? Would the constructive trust theory apply, meaning the plaintiff might have a potential chance of success? Or would the statute of frauds apply, meaning the plaintiff would have no chance of success? The answer to this one is a lawyer's favorite—it depends.

The court first needs to check constructive trust law, the nature of the pleadings, and what facts arise during

---

97. Graham v. Martin, 149 N.C. App. 831, 835–36 (N.C. Ct. App. 2002).

the trial or discovery. If the court believes that, despite how it is labeled, the case is nothing more than a mere nonperformance of an oral agreement to sell land, then there is no constructive trust.[98] Similarly, if a plaintiff merely claims that the defendant merely had an oral agreement to purchase land and then convey it to the plaintiff at the same price, this is unenforceable, and a non constructive trust theory.[99]

If the underlying case is solely based on a breach of a promise to transfer real estate to the plaintiff, then there are two ways of handling it to avoid dismissal under the statute of frauds. This is because there are two forms of constructive trust cases: one concerns a breach of a fiduciary duty, and one concerns a fraud or a wrong.

The most promising method is to use the fiduciary relationship argument. That is, the plaintiff would have to argue that, among other things, the defendant was a fiduciary of the plaintiff, and that there would be unjust enrichment if the defendant were allowed to retain the property without transferring it.[100] A careful plaintiff seeking a constructive trust would have to argue more than a mere breach of an oral promise by a person standing in close relation to the transferee; the plaintiff has to

---

98. *See* Wheelen v. Robinson, 117 N.H. 1032, 1036 (N.H. 1977); Bontecou v. Goldman, 103 A.D.2d 732, 733 (N.Y. App. Div. 1984); Mazzera v. Wolf, 30 Cal. 2d 531, 536–37 (Cal. 1947).

99. Cohn v. Jefferson Savings Loan Ass'n, 349 S.W.2d 854, 860 (Mo. 1961).

100. *See, e.g.*, Kirkland v. Handrick, 173 S.W.2d 735, 737 (Tex. Civ. App. 1943).

allege that he conveyed the property *because of* the confidential relationship.[101]

But if the underlying claim is solely breach of oral agreement, and there is no fiduciary relationship, then using the pure "fraud" or "wrong" method, is likely to be more difficult. This is in part because a breach of contract is not a "fraud" or "wrong" that constructive trust theory is designed to protect parties from. Some of these issues were implicitly addressed in an old New York Court of Appeals case, *Levy v. Brush,* in which the court held that the statute of frauds still applied to a case in which the defendant was only accused of being guilty of a fraud in refusing to perform the verbal agreement concerning the sale of real estate. This was in part because legally, there is no such thing as "fraud" in refusing to perform a contract that the law deemed unenforceable in the first place.[102] Even approximately 100 years later, the same court still held that an oral agreement cannot be the basis of a constructive trust, without the fiduciary relationship. The dissenting judge argued that so long as there is "actual fraud" and there was an "abuse of confidence reposed," then it is possible to use constructive trust theory to enforce an oral agreement. But the majority disagreed. In that particular case, the situation was unusual: plaintiff was asserting not that defendant simply agreed to convey the premises to her, but that he agreed that he would provide plaintiff with the funds to buy it and then take it off her hands at a profit to her. Instead,

---

101. *See* Farano v. Stephanelli, 7 A.D.2d 420, 424 (N.Y. App. Div. 1959).

102. 45 N.Y. 589, 591 (1871).

he actually bought it for himself and his associates, after putting her in a position where she could not make other arrangements to complete her own purchase.[103]

As indicated earlier, the statute of frauds has significant holes. And the most gaping one is a constructive trust case. Despite the preceding, in the unusual case in which the parties *do* have a written contract concerning the property at issue, in which the plaintiff formally gave up his rights on one hand, but claims there was an oral understanding outside the terms of that contract, then in that rare exception, the statute of frauds may win the day for the defendant. In other words, if the defense wishes to raise the statute of frauds not on the basis of a *lack* of a written agreement, but instead on the basis that there *is* a written agreement (especially one that cannot be modified orally), this may work as a defense. That was discussed in this chapter, section B.

103. Sutton v. Sandler, 13 N.Y.2d 1007, 1010 (1963).

Chapter 8

Laws That May Conflict with, or Be Avoided by, Constructive Trust Relief

A. Statutes of Wills and Distribution

There are potential sets of statutes that might seem to conflict with the constructive trust cause of action, in addition to ones mentioned earlier in Chapter 7, such as the statute of frauds. For example, a typical statute of wills would prevent a party from claiming that he had an oral understanding with the decedent, which was not incorporated into a signed will. But a constructive trust is an exception to such a statute. For the most part, implied trusts are not subject to the statutes of wills or statutes of descent and distribution, or statutes of inheritance.[1]

---

1. *See* Starzec v. Kida, 183 Conn. 41, 45 n.2 (1981); Bengoechea v. Bengoechea, 106 Idaho 188 n.2 (Idaho Ct. App. 1984); Voelkel v. Tohulka, 236 Ind. 588 (1957); Bastien v. Bastien, 84 A.D.2d 800 (N.Y. App. Div. 1981); Leigh v. Weiner, 679 S.W.2d 46, 48 (Tex. App. 1984); Patey v. Peaslee, 101 N.H. 26, 28–29 (N.H. 1957).

One example of how a constructive trust case can sidestep other such statutes is in *Pope v. Garrett*,[2] a Texas Supreme Court case. In that case, the court heard a claim that certain defendants had prevented a decedent from signing a certain will, and that certain relatives then obtained property by virtue of the statute of descent and distribution. That property would not have passed to them, except for the fraud and wrongful acts of other heirs, which prevented the deceased from making the will that would have passed the property to a third party. The court held that a constructive trust is not within the statute of descent and distribution or the statute of wills, and nor is it an exception to them. "It is the creature of equity." The court also held that the remedy of imposing a constructive trust "must be used with caution, especially where . . . proof of the wrongful act rests in parol, in order that it may not defeat the purposes of the statute of wills, the statute of descent and distribution, or the statute of frauds."[3] Ultimately the court did grant constructive trust relief, even against innocent parties who had no part of the wrongful acts.

Other case law helps one understand how constructive trust cases fit in with statutes about wills. For example, one case held that an implied trust may arise where a person, knowing that a testator in giving him a bequest intends that it be used for the benefit of a third party, promises to carry out the testator's intention, and then fails to do so.[4]

---

2. 147 Tex. 18 (1948).

3. *Id.* at 25.

4. Linney v. Cleveland Tr. Co., 30 Ohio App. 345 (Ohio Ct. App. 1928).

The Restatement (First) of Restitution (1937) can also be helpful to a plaintiff who seeks a constructive trust in such situations. Its section 184 provides: "Where a disposition of property by will or intestacy is procured by fraud, duress or undue influence, the person acquiring the property holds it upon a constructive trust, unless adequate relief can otherwise be given in a probate court." The comments to this section make it applicable to the situation where a decedent is, by fraud or undue influence, induced to revoke a will. The comments also indicate that the person who takes the property as a result of such a revocation "holds it upon a constructive trust for the person who would have taken under the will . . . if it had not been revoked."[5]

When it comes to the potential for constructive trusts in the context of contested wills, in certain cases the courts rule that the plaintiff can only seek to void the will, but in other cases that the plaintiff can seek a constructive trust. Sometimes the distinguishing factor is technical. In *Johnson v. Stevenson*,[6] the court held that in the context of a case in which a plaintiff argued that her brother and sister-in-law used fraudulent acts to trick her parents into executing a will that gave nothing to herself, then that plaintiff would have adequate relief in seeking a direct attack on the will. Therefore, she could not seek relief through a constructive trust. In a later case, a court from the same state heard arguments from a plaintiff who sought a constructive trust. The will of the decedent provided half of the assets to plaintiffs and half to his

5. *See also* Skidmore v. Back, 512 S.W.2d 223 (Mo. Ct. App. 1974).
6. 269 N.C. 200 (1967).

wife. The plaintiffs claimed that the defendants exercised undue influence over the deceased, gave him a pair of scissors, and convinced him to cut up his will, leaving him intestate. The result was that all of his property went to his wife, to the exclusion of the plaintiffs.[7] The court held that under those circumstances, since there was no will presented, the plaintiffs could pursue a tort remedy, and they were not limited to a probate proceeding remedy.

These rules are not necessarily universal however. In some cases a constructive trust claim will not overcome other statutes concerning wills and distribution. For example, one case in Alabama concerned an alleged deadbeat dad, whose son died. The statute provided that he would receive a portion of the proceeds from a wrongful death action, but the mother sought a constructive trust to prevent him from receiving those sums. The court held that the governing statute of distribution addressed that the damages would be issued to his parents, and that the statute allowed for no exception due to any constructive trust.[8]

B. Homestead Exemption

The homestead exemption can be very powerful. For example, a well-known felon once took advantage of Florida's extremely broad homestead exemption, and apparently never paid a dime to his victims' families, despite once owning a home there, after the families obtained a

7. Griffin v. Baucom, 74 N.C. App. 282 (N.C. Ct. App. 1985) (*disc. review denied,* 314 N.C. 115 (1985).

8. Pogue v. Pogue, 434 So. 2d 262, 263 (Ala. Civ. App. 1983).

judgment against him, in the sum of tens of millions of dollars. Can a valid constructive trust case cut through the homestead exemption law? Just like everything else in the law, it depends.

Reviewing case law is helpful to understand the general concepts. In one Iowa case, the high court held that the homestead nature of property does not shield it from the right of a constructive trustee to trace proceeds of the trust property. It also noted that if "wrongfully obtained funds" are used to purchase that property, it does not truly belong to the purchasers, and therefore, the purchasers "never acquire a homestead interest." The court went even so far as to hold that if funds are used to pay off a mortgage on the homestead, the same principle applies.[9]

The technicalities matter though. For example, in one case a lender claimed a borrower had promised to comply with statutory requirements concerning a loan that would have let the lender put a lien on the property. When the borrower did not, and the borrower claimed a homestead protection, the court refused to allow the lender to use a constructive trust theory. "To judicially impose a lien on homestead property in the form of a constructive trust based merely upon an oral promise to comply with the statutory requirements would totally undermine the homestead protection provided by the homestead provisions of the Texas statutes and constitution."[10]

9. Cox v. Waudby, 433 N.W.2d 716, 719 (Iowa 1988).

10. Matter of Daves, 770 F.2d 1363, 1367 (5th Cir. 1985).

One critical time that homestead exemptions are examined are in the context of bankruptcy proceedings. If the property at issue is subject to a constructive trust, then it is not property of the bankruptcy estate, and thus not subject to a claim of homestead exemption under bankruptcy law or applicable state law.[11]

"Traceable proceeds from prior fraudulent transfers, which are used to acquire a homestead, may also be subject to a constructive trust."[12] In one bankruptcy case, a creditor attempted to impose a constructive trust upon homestead property. In analyzing the legal principles applicable to the case, the court held that if the creditor "had proved that these properties were financed to any significant extent with money traceable to the funds embezzled by [the debtor's brother] and if it had proved that [the debtor] furnished no consideration for those funds . . . a resulting trust would be appropriate."[13] Therefore, one has to also consider what a "significant extent" of money means, in this context.

C. Bankruptcy Law and Forfeiture Law

1. Bankruptcy

One of the great benefits of a constructive trust can be seen in the context of bankruptcy cases. If your client is seeking a constructive trust against a debtor in a

11. Martin v. Jurgens (*In re* Jurgens), 620 B.R. 115, 137 n.25 (Bankr. D. Mont. 2020).

12. *In re* Fin. Federated Title & Tr., Inc., 347 F.3d 880, 891 (11th Cir. 2003).

13. *In re* Mart, 106 B.R. 309 (Bankr. S.D. Fla. 1989).

bankruptcy proceeding, he may be entitled to cut ahead of every other creditor, and get first dibs on the property at issue. That is because if the debtor is truly liable under a constructive trust theory, then the debtor does not even own the property in the first place, so it is not part of his estate. As one court put it, "any property that the debtor holds in constructive trust for another is excluded from the estate."[14] Constructive trust law cuts through all the red tape, and lets the plaintiff jump to the front of the line. A successful plaintiff in a constructive trust case has more rights than anyone else, simply because of the nature of the relief.

This result shows a tension between the goals of a constructive trust and the goals of bankruptcy law. There are at least two reasons why a bankruptcy court would prefer not to use constructive trust law. First, a constructive trust plaintiff would go to the head of the line. This is the opposite of how bankruptcy law normally works. Second, there already is a mechanism for addressing debts obtained through fraud—the statute 11 U.S.C. § 523. That statute provides the remedy of declaring nondischargeable debts arising from various types of fraud and deceit committed by the debtor.

There is a tension between the two sets of laws; although a constructive trust is generally a powerful tool, it is also what one court called "fundamentally at odds with the general goals of the Bankruptcy Code."[15] Another

---

14. *In re* Flanagan, 503 F.3d 171, 180 (2d Cir. 2007).

15. *In re* Statler & Co., 144 B.R. 385, 388 (N.D. Ill. 1992). *See also* Balgobin, 490 B.R. 13, 21 (Bankr. E.D.N.Y. 2013).

court called it "anathema to the equities of bankruptcy."[16] Bankruptcy courts are especially troubled with handling constructive trust cases because those judges presumably have a natural bias in favor of focusing on bankruptcy law rather than constructive trust law.

There is no magical black and white approach that all bankruptcy courts follow. However a general rule seems to be that the bankruptcy courts rule that a constructive trust should be imposed only if there is "a substantial reason to do so."[17] To put it another way, the bankruptcy courts generally disfavor the idea of applying constructive trust law, and act cautiously about applying it.[18] One court held that "it may be harder to get a constructive trust ruling from some bankruptcy courts than for a camel to pass through the eye of a needle."[19]

Because constructive trusts are disfavored in bankruptcy cases, a plaintiff claiming he is entitled to such relief should be ready to prove a fraud that could not be remedied through traditional bankruptcy law, extreme injustice, or egregious conduct. One case held that "[T]he grounds for imposing a constructive trust

16. *In re* Omegas Grp., Inc. 16 F.3d 1443, 1452 (6th Cir. 1994); *see also* Flanagan v. Mangan, 503 F.3d 171, 180 (2d Cir. 2007) (noting that the effect of a constructive trust within bankruptcy is "profound").

17. *See In re* Balgobin, 490 B.R. 13, 21 (Bankr. E.D.N.Y. 2013); *Flanagan,* 503 F.3d 171.

18. *See, e.g., In re* WEB2B Payment Solutions, Inc., 815 F.3d 400, 407 (8th Cir. 2016) ("courts are reluctant to impost post-petition constructive trusts"); *In re* Ades & Berg Grp. Investors, 550 F.3d 240, 245, 247 (2d Cir. 2008); *In re* Ross, 478 B.R. 715, 731 (Bankr. W.D.N.C. 2012).

19. WAS, LLC v. Coll (*In re* DC Energy, LLC), 555 B.R. 786, 791 (Bankr. D.N.M. 2016).

must be so clear, convincing, strong and unequivocal as to lead to but one conclusion."[20]

A non constructive trust creditor has a plethora of case law to rely on in order to try to put a constructive trust plaintiff at the back of the line. But there is case law indicating that parties do have the right to allege a constructive trust case against a debtor in a bankruptcy case. As Justice Black held in *Pearlman v. Reliance Insurance Co.*, "The Bankruptcy Act simply does not authorize a trustee to distribute other people's property among a bankrupt's creditors."[21] As one bankruptcy court noted, "If a constructive trust is recognized in appropriate circumstances, then the trust *res* really is 'other people's property' and should not be used to pay the debtor's creditors."[22] Recognizing a constructive trust in a bankruptcy case prevents unjust enrichment to other creditors by excluding property to which those creditors would have had no claim outside bankruptcy. This is because "Congress did not mean to authorize a bankruptcy estate to benefit from property that the debtor did not own."[23]

Depending on circumstances, a clever attorney can use other arguments to try to convince a bankruptcy court that his client should have access to the property at issue. For example, a bankruptcy estate "does not include

---

20. Amendola v. Bayer, 907 F.2d 760, 763 (7th Cir. 1990); *see also In re* Builders Capital & Services, Inc., 317 B.R. 603, 612 (Bankr. W.D.N.Y. 2004); *In re* Coffman, 273 B.R. 137, 138 (Bankr. S.D. Ohio 2001).

21. 371 U.S. 132, 135–36 (1962).

22. Marcus v. Horton (*In re* Horton), 618 B.R. 22, 26 (Bankr. D.N.M. 2020).

23. Vineyard v. McKenzie (*In re* Quality Holstein Leasing), 752 F.2d 1009, 1013 (5th Cir. 1985).

property of others in which the debtor has some minor interest such as a . . . bare legal title."[24] A relevant bankruptcy law statute reads as follows: "Property in which the debtor holds, as of the commencement of the case, only legal title and not an equitable interest . . . becomes property of the estate only to the extent of the debtor's legal title to such property, but not to the extent of any equitable interest in such property that the debtor does not hold."[25] Therefore, a plaintiff may want to focus the court's attention as to whether the estate really and truly "holds" the property at issue. Alternatively, an attorney may want to focus on the kind of competing creditors at issue, and whether they really should be treated equally to the plaintiff in question. That is, after all, the main reason why bankruptcy courts discourage the use of constructive trusts. They naturally have an "all creditors are created equal" mindset, so if there is a way of showing that does not apply, the plaintiff will have an advantage.

2. Forfeiture

In an unusual situation, and attorney might have a client seeking a constructive trust when the property at issue is subject to forfeiture. A large majority of courts have determined (1) that a constructive trust despite being an equitable remedy, constitutes a "legal right, title, or interest in . . . property" under the federal statute that allows one to make a claim for reimbursement of the property forfeited to the government and (2) that a constructive

---

24. *In re* Balgobin, 490 B.R. 13, 20 (Bankr. E.D.N.Y. 2013).
25. 11 U.S.C. § 541(d).

trust can potentially render a forfeiture order invalid.[26] This law is not universal. One court got hypertechnical and held that a constructive trust "is a *remedy* that a court devises after litigation," and therefore it cannot "be interposed as superior to the government's forfeiture claim" because forfeiture vests title in the government at the time of the defendant's wrongdoing.[27]

---

26. *See, e.g.*, United States v. Shefton, 548 F.3d 1360, 1365 (11th Cir. 2008), citing, inter alia, United States v. $4,224,958.57, 392 F.3d 1002, 1004–05 (9th Cir. 2004); United States v. Schmmmer, 968 F.2d 1570, 1574, 1582 (2d Cir. 1992); United States v. Campos, 859 F.2d 1233, 1238–39 (6th Cir. 1988).

27. United States v. BCCI Holdings (Luxembourg), S.A., 46 F.3d 1185, 1190–91 (D.C. Cir. 1995).

Chapter 9

Alternatives to a Constructive Trust

A. Equitable Lien

As seen from Chapter 2, section C, there are times in which a plaintiff never owned the property but allegedly spent his own time, money, sweat, blood, and tears into improving the property or otherwise keeping it afloat. Although the first instinct would be to deem this a constructive trust case and have your client seek the entirety of the property, it would be too early at the pleading stage to restrict oneself to just that form of relief. This would be especially the case if (1) the plaintiff's time, money, or sweat equity were relatively limited, or (2) the case is being heard in New York.

Instead of merely seeking a constructive trust, for this kind of case the plaintiff should also strongly consider seeking an equitable lien, as a kind of backup plan. The difference between a constructive trust and an equitable lien can be found in the Restatement (First) of Restitution (1937). As previously indicated in the Introduction, according to section 160 of that Restatement, the constructive trust arises when the person holding title has an equitable duty to transfer that plaintiff. This gives a plaintiff potential title to the property. In contrast, an equitable lien exists as a "security for a claim" and typically arises when an individual makes improvements on the land of another.[1]

An equitable lien is a kind of constructive trust, but just a limited one. An equitable lien is enforced by foreclosing on it, and ultimately obtaining a money payment, as opposed to obtaining full title to the premises. At the very least, though, an equitable lien affords a preference over other creditors.[2] Many courts use the terms "equitable lien" and "constructive trust" interchangeably, which makes the subject even more confusing.

In New York, "an equitable lien may be imposed where one in a confidential relationship with the owner has expended money for improvement of the property based on a promise to convey, reimburse, or grant a lesser interest in the property."[3] At least one court has indicated that an essential element of an equitable lien upon real property "is that the improver of the property made such improvements in good faith and under a

---

1. Restatement (First) of Restitution (1937) § 161, cmt. a.

2. *See* Leyden v. Citicorp Indus. Bank, 782 P.2d 6, 10 n.8, citing D. Dobbs, Remedies § 4.3, at 249 (1973).

3. Bolender v. Ronin Prop. Partners, LLC, 168 A.D.3d 1032, 1035 (N.Y. App. Div. 2019).

color of right."[4] In Illinois, it is described as "a remedy for a debt that cannot be legally enforced, but which ought in right and fairness to be recognized."[5] The same court held that in order to impose an equitable lien, a plaintiff must prove "(1) a debt, duty or obligation owed to it by the defendant, and (2) the existence of a *res* that, in some way, is particularly related to the debt or obligation."[6] In Missouri, the elements are "(1) a duty or an obligation owing by one person to another; (2) a *res* to which that obligation fastens, which can be identified or described with reasonable certainty; and (3) an intent, express or implied, that the property serve as security for the payment of the debt or obligation."[7]

In New York, there are two distinct types of equitable liens.[8] The first type is focused on preventing unjust enrichment. This equitable lien can be created when a party standing in confidential relationship with the legal owner of the property makes payments from his or her own funds toward the purchase price, reduction of the mortgage or improvements to the real property under circumstances that would entitle that party to restitution. For this kind of equitable lien, the party must present a clear intent between the parties that such property be held, given, or transferred as security for an obligation.

---

4. Rodriguez v. Fed Nat'l Mortg. Assn. Index No. 508453/2019 (N.Y. Sup. Ct. 2020), citing Mickles v. Dillaye, 17 N.Y. 80 (1858).

5. Paliatka v. Bush, 109 N.E.3d 343, 351 (Ill. App. Ct. 2018) (citation omitted).

6. *Id.*

7. Ethridge v. Tierone Bank, 226 S.W.3d 127, 134 (Mo. 2007).

8. Angel v. Strulovich, 2020 N.Y. slip op. 33975, 13–15 (N.Y. Sup. Ct. 2020).

The second type is where debt is owed but no agreement is in place and equity demands certain property stand as security for payment for the debt. As explained by one commentator,

> for example, if *A* defrauds *B* out of $1,000, and uses the money to buy a car, *B* might seek the equitable remedies of constructive trust or equitable lien. If *A*'s wrongdoing was so egregious to merit the imposition of a constructive trust, *A* essentially will be deprived of any right to the car, but will instead be deemed to hold it for *B*'s benefit. Therefore, if *A* sells the car for $2,000, *A* will lose the benefit of the $1,000 appreciation. Conversely, if *B* only gets an equitable lien, if *A* sells the car for $2,000, the first $1,000 goes to *B*, and *A* gets the benefit of the other $1,000.[9]

B. Resulting Trust

A close sibling to a constructive trust is known as a "resulting trust." Some courts consider it an identical twin, not distinguishing between the two. And some courts, such as those in New York, hardly refer to such trusts at all, apparently lumping them in the same category as constructive trusts.[10]

---

9. *Id.*, citing Advanced Chapter Eleven Bankruptcy Practice § 6.45, Equitable Liens and Constructive Trusts Asserted Against Real Property as They Relate to the Trustee's Strong-arm Powers, n.14 (2d ed., 2020-2 Cumulative Supplement).

10. Walwyn v. U.S., 51 F. Supp. 2d 320, 322 (E.D.N.Y. 1999).

Generally a "resulting trust" is one in which the parties intend to create the trust relationship but do not execute documents or establish adequate evidence of the intent. The typical case is where the money man/beneficiary puts up the money to buy land but has a second person listed as the title holder. If there is a resulting trust, the second person, the named owner, is really holding it for the benefit of the unnamed beneficiary. By contrast, a constructive trust is a relationship adjudicated to exist based on particular factual situations created by the parties. The parties do not necessarily need to "intend" to set up a constructive trust. It is simply that the court "constructs" the trust as a matter of equity to avoid unjust enrichment, typically because of such matters discussed previously, like fraud, undue influence, abuse of confidence, or mistake in the transaction that originates the problem.[11]

There are three factual circumstances in which a resulting trust can arise: "(1) where an express trust fails in whole or in part; (2) where an express trust is fully performed without exhausting the trust estate; [or] (3) where property is purchased and the purchase price is paid by one person and at his direction the vendor conveys the property to another person."[12] A resulting trust originating from the first two circumstances is not described here, because those circumstances arise only where there is an express trust, but its terms do not

11. *See* Wadlington v. Edwards, 92 So. 2d 629, 632 (Fla. 1957).

12. Saulia v. Saulia, 31 A.D.2d 640 (N.Y. App. Div. 1968) (quoting 4 Scott, Trusts [2d ed.], § 404.1, at 2922).

provide for what should happen if the trust fails or if there is a surplus.[13]

The third scenario is known as a "purchase-money resulting trust," in which the property is held in trust by the title holder for the person who paid the purchase price. This is the primary kind at issue in this section. In such a case, the nominal title holder is said to hold the property in trust for the benefit of the person who paid the consideration based on the "natural presumption that, in the absence of anything to show the contrary, he who supplies the purchase price intends that the property bought shall inure to his own benefit and not that of another, and that the conveyance is taken in the name of another for some incidental reason."[14]

If one person pays for the property, and the property is taken in the name of another, and the person paying the sums is seeking to enforce his intent for an undocumented agreement, then the case concerns their mutual original intent. Some courts indicate that in that case, a resulting trust is the appropriate procedural vehicle.[15]

The concept for a resulting trust is that there is a "'natural equity' that the one who pays for the property should enjoy it."[16] Many cases involve title to real property being transferred to a family member, paid for by

---

13. *See* Geltzer v. Balgobin (*In re* Balgobin) 490 B.R. 13, 27 (Bankr. E.D.N.Y. 2013) (citation omitted).

14. Quinn v. Quinn, 260 Mass. 494, 501 (Mass. 1927).

15. *See* Soles v. Stevenson, 53 Misc.2d 402 (N.Y. Sup. Ct. 1967); Zack v. Guzauskas, 171 Conn. 98, 103 (Conn. 1976).

16. *In re* Estate of Koch, 297 Ill. App. 3d 786 (Ill. App. Ct. 1998).

their parents, for some purpose other than a gift or to convey ownership.[17]

In many other respects, resulting trusts are treated similarly to constructive trusts. For example, they are not within the statute of frauds, and may be proved by parol evidence.[18] In addition, the burden is still on the person "seeking to establish the trust, and that person must provide clear, convincing and unmistakable evidence to support his theory."[19] There are some exceptions to that; burdens in a constructive trust case and resulting trust case are covered in Chapter 11.

A critical issue for a resulting trust is whether the one paying for the property intended to make a gift, or whether he intended to be deemed a title holder. Some courts cite the Restatement (Second) of Trusts: "[w]here a transfer of property is made to one person and the purchase price is paid by another, a resulting trust arises in favor of the person by whom the purchase price is paid [with certain exceptions]."[20] One exception is that no resulting trust arises "if the person by whom the purchase price is paid manifests an intention that no resulting trust should arise."[21] The Restatement also indicates that it is critical to see who received the property, in order

17. *See* Johnson v. Johnson, 192 Cal. App. 3d 551 (Cal. Ct. App. 1987); McCosker v. McCosker, 122 Cal. App. 2d 498 (Cal. Ct. App. 1954).

18. *See* Jahnigen v. Smith, 143 Md. App. 547, 557–58 (Md. Ct. Spec. App. 2002); Williams v. Com. Tr. Co., 276 Mass. 508, 517 (Mass. 1931).

19. Scanlon v. Scanlon, 6 Ill. 2d 224, 230 (1955).

20. Restatement (Second) of Trusts § 440 (1959).

21. *Id.* § 441.

to determine whether there is a gift or a trust that was set up.[22]

New York passed a statute entitled "Purchase-money resulting trust abolished,"[23] which on its face appears to have abolished resulting trusts. But the exceptions to the statute are big enough to allow for relief in many cases. "A resulting trust may still be established if (1) title to property is taken in the name of one person without the consent or knowledge of the person who paid a consideration for the transfer, or (2) in violation of a trust, the transferee has purchased property with the money of another person."[24]

There is also some case law indicating that bankruptcy courts treat resulting trusts differently from constructive trusts. One case held that although a constructive trust could be part of a debtor's estate, "[a] transaction that has failed to carry out the parties' intent becomes a resulting trust, and a resulting trust cannot be part of the debtor's estate."[25]

---

22. *Id.* § 442.

23. EPTL 7-1.3(a).

24. Mendel v. Hewitt, 161 A.D.2d 849, 851 (N.Y. App. Div. 1990).

25. *In re* Golden Triangle Capital, Inc., 171 B.R. 79, 82 (B.A.P. 9th Cir. 1994).

Chapter 10

Special Benefits of a Constructive Trust Case

A. Preliminary Injunctive Relief

A constructive trust case is an equitable action, which means one may seek injunctive relief. One form of potential relief is a preliminary injunction, preventing the trustee from disposing of the property pending the outcome of the case. This is true even if the underlying action seeks a specific fund of money. However, if your client is seeking monetary damages, then it may be difficult or impossible to convince a court to restrain the defendant from spending those funds during the pendency of the case. Sometimes this seems like simply a technical difference in nomenclature and the form of the lawsuit, but the end result can be a difference of night and day.

The best way to understand the difference is to review cases. On the tough end is *Credit Agricole Indosuez v. Rossiyskiy Kredit Bank,*[1] in which the plaintiffs, which were foreign banking institutions, commenced an action seeking to recover unsecured debts of the defendants totaling $30 million. The New York Court of Appeals (its highest court) denied the plaintiffs' motion for a preliminary injunction to prevent a defendant banking institution from transferring or conveying assets necessary to satisfy any judgment awarded to the plaintiffs. The Court of Appeals indicated that "an unsecured creditor suing to collect a debt [is] not entitled to preliminary injunctive relief to prevent the debtor's dissipation of assets prior to judgment."[2] In reaching that conclusion, the Court of Appeals relied on the principles that provisional injunctive relief is typically limited to equitable actions where the defendant threatened to violate the rights of the plaintiff respecting the subject of the action, which would tend to render the judgment ineffectual. It noted that a plaintiff in an action seeking a money judgment "has no rights as against the property of the defendant until he obtains a judgment."[3]

Conversely, in one California case, plaintiffs, stockholders in Walt Disney Productions, sought to recover the payoff in the greenmailing of that corporation. One of the defendants was an entity to whom the greenmail, approximately $325 million, was paid.[4] For those of us who read this and had no idea what a "greenmailer" was,[5] the court

1. 94 N.Y.2d 541 (2000).

2. *Id.* at 546 (citation omitted).

3. *Id.* at 546–47 (citation omitted).

4. Heckmann v. Ahmanson, 168 Cal. App. 3d 119 (Cal. Ct. App. 1985).

5. Like me.

explained that "a greenmailer creates the threat of a corporate takeover by purchasing a significant amount of the company's stock. He then sells the shares back to the company at a premium when its executives, in fear of their jobs, agree to buy him out."[6] The plaintiffs claimed that the greenmailer's profit from the transaction, approximately $60 million, should be kept in trust, and that the greenmailer was obligated to render periodic accountings of the disposition of the entire proceeds.

The greenmailer argued that the plaintiffs had an adequate remedy at law in the form of money damages, especially as there was no serious question as to the solvency of any of the defendants. The court disagreed, holding that this was irrelevant. The court also noted that even if theoretically potential money damages would ordinarily be sufficient to bar constructive trust relief (and a preliminary injunction), the plaintiffs had a specific reason for being entitled to such relief. That is, since the plaintiffs were entitled to trace the funds to its ultimate product or profit, then "by the time plaintiff obtains a final judgment, the original fund may have grown far greater than the legal rate of interest would recognize. To allow the defendant to pocket the difference would reward the defendant for his wrongdoing."[7]

A preliminary injunction can also be useful in the event that, for whatever reason, a lis pendens is not available. As indicated later in this chapter, a lis pendens is ordinarily available for real estate at issue in a constructive

6. 168 Cal. App. 3d at 123.

7. *Id.* at 135.

trust case. But of course, not all property held by a potential trustee would be real estate.

Of course, one does not simply obtain a preliminary injunction by asking for it. In New York, for example, to establish entitlement to a preliminary injunction, a movant must establish (1) a probability of success on the merits, (2) irreparable harm in the absence of an injunction, and (3) a balance of the equities in favor of granting the injunction. The second and third prongs should be relatively easy to prove in a legitimate constructive trust case. That is because (1) a constructive trust depends (in many cases) on the concept that money damages would not compensate the plaintiff, and (2) a decent constructive trust case would already be based on the idea that the equities are in the plaintiff's favor.

The first prong, likelihood of success, may be a tougher one. While some cases indicate that a "prima facie" case is strong enough to warrant immediate relief, other cases take the "likelihood of success" standard more strictly. And a good defense to a preliminary injunction request would be for the defendant to explain that the burden in a constructive trust case is already clear and convincing, and therefore the standard to prove "likelihood of success" should similarly be a higher one compared to an average case.

One critical issue for a preliminary injunction is that, in some jurisdictions, the court must compel the plaintiff to provide an undertaking, meaning funds or a bond to be deposited with the court in the event that the injunction was improperly issued. This is another way that a defendant can try to get away with avoiding injunctive relief.

B. The Right to Profits

Since a constructive trust is an equitable cause of action, one can potentially get the benefit of equitable relief. One form of equitable relief is disgorgement of profits.[8]

As indicated otherwise in this book, a successful constructive trust case would permit the plaintiff to obtain a return of the property. But that is not all. In the right kind of case, a plaintiff could also be entitled to the profits the defendant earned with that property. And that is regardless of whether the plaintiff would have been able, or had any intention, to earn a profit with the same piece of property. "[A] constructive trust beneficiary may obtain, through tracing, not merely what was lost but also other property or profits traceable to that lost property."[9] This right to profits makes a constructive trust distinct from, for example, an equitable trust cause of action.

The Restatement of Restitution addresses this right to profit implicitly. If a wrongdoer exchanges misappropriated property for other property, the plaintiff can obtain that new property. Section 202 provides: "Where a person wrongfully disposes of property of another knowing that the disposition is wrongful and acquires in exchange other property, the other is entitled . . . to enforce . . . a constructive trust of the property so

---

8. *See* Feltner v. Columbia Pictures Television, Inc., 523 U.S. 340, 352 (1998) (observing that the Supreme Court has described "actions for disgorgement of improper profits" as "equitable"); Tull v. United States, 481 U.S. 412, 424 (1987) (stating that "an action for disgorgement of improper profits" is "traditionally considered an equitable remedy").

9. *In re* Marriage of Allen, 724 P.2d 651, 656 (Colo. 1986).

acquired." In essence, this means that if, for example, a defendant improperly takes control of a $1 million property, waits for the market to go up, and then in essence exchanges that old property for a new $2 million property, the plaintiff should be entitled to that new property worth $2 million.

Several courts have explained the reason for allowing a plaintiff to recover profits. For example, a California court indicated that if a defendant retained profits after successfully engaging in greenmailing, then this would "reward the defendant for his own wrongdoing."[10]

One example of how this works is in the U.S. Supreme Court case *Snepp v. United States*,[11] also described elsewhere in this book. In that case, upon accepting employment in the CIA, Snepp had an alleged fiduciary obligation not to publish information relating to the Agency's activities without first obtaining Agency approval. Regardless, he published a book about CIA activities in South Vietnam without that approval. The Court held in essence that the United States had a constructive trust over the royalties from the book. Notably, it was of no concern to the Court that the United States presumably would never have planned to use that same information to publish its own book, to make royalties. That was a non-issue.

Another somewhat related example would be in the context of an employer–employee relationship. Since an employee is required to act with loyalty to the employer,

10. Heckmann v. Ahmanson, 168 Cal. App. 3d 119, 135 (Cal. Ct. App. 1985).

11. 444 U.S. 507 (1980).

then an employee who makes a profit or receives a benefit in connection with transactions conducted by him on behalf of his employer is under a duty to give such profit or benefit to his employer, whether or not it was received by the employee in violation of his duty of loyalty. As the New York Court of Appeals held in such a case, "any compensation secretly or improperly received from others beyond the compensation to which the employee is entitled is deemed to be held by him on a constructive trust for his employer."[12] A another court put it, "A court may construct a remedy when an employee profits through a breach of fiduciary duty by imposing a constructive trust on the employer's profits."[13]

In litigating the issue, it is a good idea to include in the complaint a request for an "accounting for profits." As one court put it, "An accounting is imposed when the property subject to the constructive trust produces profits while in the defendant's possession." The same court went on to indicate that for the accounting relief, an accounting does not seek any particular res or fund of money. Instead, the defendant simply must provide profits he had obtained, even if they were not necessarily kept in a special account dedicated to the particular res at issue.[14]

The profits a successful plaintiff is entitled to do not have to be ones earned by the defendant. They could also include lost potential profits. For example, in one Illinois

---

12. Western Elec. Co. v. Brenner, 41 N.Y.2d 291, 295 (1977).

13. Wall Sys., Inc. v. Pompa, 324 Conn. 718, 742 (Conn. 2017) (citations and internal brackets omitted). This reference to "employer's" may have meant "employee's."

14. Parke v. First Reliance Standard Life Ins. Co., 368 F.3d 999, 1008 (8th Cir. 2004).

case, the court not only awarded constructive trust relief, but also awarded plaintiff money damages. Those sums, represented the farming profits he would have earned had defendants not refused to convey the real property. Although defendants claimed the proper measure of damages was just the fair market rental value, the Illinois Supreme Court disagreed. It analogized the situation to a breach of duty between a principal and agent. It implicitly held that this was a valid basis to compel the defendant to pay for lost profits.[15]

An employee who is willing to play a dirty trick, and wants a nice quick way to success, may steal customer lists when he leaves his former business, as a means of starting a new business. In the right kind of case, even if damages (including lost profits) resulting from the breach of loyalty would "compensate" the plaintiff, the court can award more. It can also issue a constructive trust on the wrongfully obtained profits from the defendants who profited from the breach of loyalty. This is because of the "wise public policy that, for the purpose of removing all temptation, extinguishes all possibility of profit flowing from a breach of the confidence imposed by the fiduciary relation." In certain kinds of cases, only "a total disgorgement" of profits "would recognize the seriousness of the wrongdoing."[16]

One can also make a kind of "profit" by engaging in insider trading. Disgorging that profit can be included as the relief in a constructive trust case. For example,

---

15. Ray v. Winter, 67 Ill. 2d 296, 306–07 (Ill. 1977).

16. *See* Hill v. Names Addresses, Inc., 212 Ill. App. 3d 1065, 1083 (Ill. App. Ct. 1991) (citations omitted).

in the New York case *Tsutsui v. Barasch*,[17] the court held that insider trading by a corporate officer is a breach of a fiduciary duty. And even though the trading "does not always cause a direct harm to the corporation, it is the corporation that has the higher claim to profits resulting from the use of inside information which has been entrusted to a fiduciary."[18] The court held that in such a case, "equity requires the imposition of a constructive trust over any profits gained from the use of such information in order to prevent an unjust enrichment."[19]

If one's client is the defendant, presuming he is caught dead to rights in breach of a fiduciary duty, there are at least some potential arguments to be made to avoid disgorging profits. One could be that it was not merely the breach of the fiduciary duty that brought the defendant riches—you can claim it was also the defendant's shrewd business decisions. Whether this kind of argument would be partially or completely successful perhaps depends on whether the court's inclination is to stamp out all possible breaches of duties, and whether the court believes that the breach was a relatively minor part of the reason the defendant obtained his profits.

C. Notice of Pendency

Many constructive trust cases concern real property. If so, it is critical that the attorney file a notice of pendency also known as a lis pendens. A lis pendens is permitted

17. 67 A.D.3d 896, 898–99 (N.Y. App. Div. 2009).

18. *Id.* at 899.

19. *Id.*

only when the action actually "affect[s] the title to real property."[20]

A lis pendens is not technically a lien; it is just a notice to the world that a lawsuit exists concerning a dispute of ownership. (Most nonattorneys describe it as a "lien," and most attorneys do not consider it worth the effort to explain the difference.) In any event, it usually does deter others from buying such property or allowing it to be refinanced, because it means the ownership rights are in question, and the new lender or purchaser takes it subject to the rights of the one filing the lis pendens. Once the lis pendens is recorded, then so long as it is effective, all persons who thereafter deal with the property are bound by all rulings of the court in the litigation.

A notice of pendency allows a party claiming an interest in real property to implicitly notify prospective purchasers or encumbrancers that the property at issue is the subject of litigation. This is crucial because if a bona fide purchaser purchases the property without knowledge of the suit, and the proceeds are dissipated, it may be impossible for even a successful plaintiff to obtain actual relief.

The New York Civil Practice Law and Rules section 6501 provides, in relevant part, that a "notice of pendency may be filed in any action in a court of the state or of the United States in which the judgment demanded would affect the title to, or the possession, use or enjoyment of, real property." A notice is filed in the office of the clerk of any county where the affected property is

---

20. Pond Place Partners, Inc. v. Poole, 351 S.C. 1, 17–18 (S.C. Ct. App.2002) (citation omitted).

located, and must state only (1) the names of the parties to the court action to which it relates, (2) the object of the action, and (3) a description of the property affected. In New York, the summons must be served on the defendant within 30 days after the lis pendens is filed.[21] Whatever state an attorney is in, he should be careful about filing it 100 percent properly. The right to a lis pendens is described as "an extraordinary privilege granted by statute," which means that "strict compliance with the statutory provisions is required."[22]

New York has an unusual quirk; the notice of pendency officially has a shelf life of only three years. (This makes it unlike a notice of pendency in, say Texas or California, which lasts for the entire litigation. In Texas, "[a] lis pendens operates only during the pendency of the [underlying] suit, and only as to those matters that are involved in the suit. It terminates with the judgment, in the absence of an appeal.")[23]

Therefore, a New York attorney handling such a case has only a few choices. First, finish the entire case within a three-year period. Second, have the notice of pendency extended before it expires. Third, allow the notice of pendency to expire. Although the latter method appears to be extremely dangerous, just because three years have elapsed since a notice of pendency has been filed does not mean a title company would ignore the old notice of pendency. Any decent title insurer would still report it to a prospective purchaser or lender, who in turn would

---

21. N.Y. CPLR 6512.

22. *Id.* at 17.

23. *Rosborough v. Cook*, 108 Tex. 364, 367 (1917).

likely refuse to enter into any transaction with such radioactive property.

There are also risks with filing a frivolous case, or not pursuing the case in good faith. In such a case, an aggrieved property owner can not only seek to have the lis pendens dismissed, but they require the plaintiff to pay any costs arising out of the filing of the notice of pendency and its cancellation by the court, and also "any costs of the action."[24] In theory, this could include the defendant's attorneys' fees. In theory, it could also mean damages suffered due to the inability to transfer the property for a high price during the pendency of the case. California similarly has a statute indicating that if the lis pendens is not proper, the owner of the property may be able to recover attorneys' fees and costs for the cost of bringing a motion to remove the lis pendens.[25]

However, at least in New York, because a notice of pendency is an "undeniably true statement," a defendant cannot maintain a successful case for slander of title.[26]

If there is no legitimate basis for a constructive trust case, and the plaintiff simply uses those words in the complaint, that should not be enough, even in a liberal state like New York. "The cases hold that a notice of *lis pendens* cannot be filed where the party who has filed it claims no right, title or interest in or to the real estate against which it is filed, and where the suit concerns simply some" improper act like an encroachment.[27]

---

24. N.Y. CPLR 6514(c).

25. *See* CAL. CODE CIV. PROC. § 405.30, 405.38.

26. Brown v. Bethlehem Terrace, 136 A.D.2d 222 (N.Y. App. Div. 1988).

27. Braunston v. Anchorage Woods, Inc., 10 N.Y.2d 302, 305 (1961).

Courts outside New York are at times more restrictive in what cases warrant a lis pendens. The California legislature enacted Code of Civil Procedure section 405.4, which intentionally left the phrase "real property claim" vague, leaving it to the courts to determine whether a claim supporting a constructive trust will justify the maintenance of a lis pendens. One court held that it must be decided on a "case-by-case basis," and that "the courts have been restrictive because of well-known dangers that the lis pendens procedure can be abused to coerce a defendant to settle a claim. The courts have looked to the substance of the dispute to determine whether it is 'essentially' a fraud action seeking money damages, with constructive trust allegations 'appended.'"[28]

In Texas, one court noted an example of when a lis pendens is appropriate, and when it is not, for a constructive trust case. The court held that if the plaintiff's pleadings sought a constructive trust for a piece of property and sought an interest in that property, the notice of lis pendens against that property would be valid. Conversely, if a party sought relief because the adversary had allegedly converted real property and used the proceeds to buy other properties, a notice of pendency against the newly purchased property would be invalid. That is because the plaintiffs in effect would only be seeking a constructive trust in order to satisfy a judgment they might obtain against the defendant.[29]

---

28. BGJ Assoc., LLC v. Super. Ct., 75 Cal. App. 4th 952, 971–72 (Cal. Ct. App. 1999).

29. First Nat'l Petroleum v. Lloyd, 908 S.W.2d 23, 25 (Tex. App. 1995).

Chapter 11

Trial Issues

A. Burden

A constructive trust is a powerful tool; it lets one potentially obtain real property by arguing parol evidence, without worrying about the statute of frauds. It also puts a plaintiff ahead of all other creditors for the property or funds at issue. But it comes at a price: the degree of evidence necessary to prove one's case.

One court noted that "this liberality [in permitting use of parol evidence] is counterbalanced by the rigid standard of proof which equity decrees as a prerequisite to the establishment of a constructive trust."[1] One of the reasons for this heavy burden is that there is generally "a policy favoring security of title and ownership, as well as a reluctance to forge beyond the grantor's apparent intent in order to work a divestiture at equity."[2]

---

1. Whitmire v. Adams, 273 S.C. 453, 458 (1979).
2. Hopwood v. Pickett, 145 N.H. 207, 209 (2000).

A plaintiff seeking to claim a constructive trust generally requires clear and convincing evidence, rather than a mere preponderance. One court described it as follows: "To establish a constructive trust, an extraordinary degree of proof is required. The evidence must be unquestionable in character. The evidence must be so clear, cogent, and convincing as to exclude every reasonable doubt in the mind of the trial court."[3] Another court described the rule as requiring "an extraordinary degree of certainty and clarity."[4]

There are a number of critical exceptions to this rule about burdens. If the constructive trust case does not concern one in which someone showed an apparent intent to transfer title or ownership to another, then one might have a good argument that the clear and convincing standard does not apply. For example, if the case concerns stolen customer lists, and the former employer is seeking a constructive trust over that list and the profits obtained by that list, potentially the burden would not apply.

An offbeat example of when the burden does not apply is a slayer case—for example when a son murders his father in order to obtain the insurance proceeds, or to inherit his assets.[5] In the cases that apply a constructive trust analysis to a slayer case, then once the murder has been proven, the remaining issues, such as whether it is "unjust" to allow the killer to keep those funds, do not need clear and convincing evidence. The rationale

3. Fix v. Fix, 847 S.W.2d 762, 765 (Mo. 1993).

4. Barriffe v. Estate of Nelson, 153 So. 3d 613, 618 (Miss. 2014) (citation omitted).

5. A private message to my kids—don't test this one out.

for the clear and convincing evidence standard does not apply.[6]

(A famous slayer case in which the murderer did not have the right to inherit, despite being named in the will, was the case of Jean Harris, who killed her lover Herman Tarnower, a well-known cardiologist and author of the best-selling fad book *The Complete Scarsdale Medical Diet.* That book has this unfortunate quote in the acknowledgments page: "We are grateful to Jean Harris for her splendid assistance in the research and writing of this book.")

If the constructive trust is based on a breach of fiduciary theory, that is, that the fiduciary received property from the plaintiff, then the burden issue sometimes moves like a pinball, to the point where it becomes extremely difficult to keep track of who has the burden. This is made even more difficult because of confusing and inconsistent case law. Regardless, one way of explaining it is as follows.

The plaintiff would first have to prove the grantor transferred something to a grantee, and that they had a fiduciary relationship or confidential relationship, or the grantee dealt from a position of overpowering influence as to the subordinate party. These kinds of issues would have to be proven by clear and convincing evidence. However, once the plaintiff hits this burden, then many courts will deem it a presumptively fraudulent transaction, and presumptively the result of undue influence. If such a relationship is found to exist, the burden of proof should shift to the grantee to (1) negate a presumption of undue influence, and (2) prove that all aspects

6. Hopwood v. Pickett, 145 N.H. 207, 209 (2000).

of the transaction were and that all was fair, open, voluntary, and well understood by clear, convincing, and satisfactory evidence.[7] As another court put it, once the confidential relationship is proven, it is "upon the profiting fiduciary the burden of showing the fairness of the transactions."[8] Another court held similarly that once a confidential relationship has been established, the party opposing a constructive trust has the burden of negating the constructive trust by clear and convincing evidence.[9]

Critically for attorneys (and who else would read this book?) the burden could have a nasty effect on an attorney having a business relationship with a client, if that attorney becomes a defendant in a constructive trust case. An attorney has a "special relationship" with a client, and therefore if the attorney is accused of doing something unfair, the attorney will have the burden to "prove complete good faith and the total absence of fraud or overreaching." Otherwise, he may be found to have breached his fiduciary duty.[10]

However, before one gets too excited about this potential switch in burdens, there is some confusion about whether it applies in the context of a family relationship. In some cases, transfers between family members are still subject to this same rule, meaning the donee

---

7. *See* Mendenhall v. Judy, 671 N.W.2d 452, 454–55 (Iowa 2003); Scribner v. Gibbs, 953 N.E.2d 475, 484–85 (Ind. Ct. App. 2011); Gordon v. Bialystoker Center & Bikur Cholim, Inc., 45 N.Y.2d 692, 698–99 (1978); Hofert v. Latorri, 22 Ill. 2d 126, 130 (1961).

8. Tex. Bank & Tr. Co. v. Moore, 595 S.W.2d 502, 509 (Tex. 1980).

9. Hieble v. Hieble, 164 Conn. 56, 62 (1972).

10. B C Investors v. Vojak, 79 So. 3d 42, 47 (Fla. Dist. Ct. App. 2011) (citations omitted).

would have to prove the transaction is fair, especially if their connection is beyond a mere family relationship.[11] In others, the court holds there is no presumption of undue influence just because there is a close family relationship, and instead the court implicitly notes that it is normal for family members to give each other gifts.[12]

A careful practitioner may have to sift through a good deal of his or her own state's case law, some of which may be inconsistent with other cases, about family members. If all else fails, and the donor wants to prove that he did not mean to truly give his property to a family member "for keeps," then it would be best if that donor can prove that the relationship went beyond a simple family relationship. If the donor can prove either that the donor had trouble understanding the nature of the transfer, or that the donor had such trust in the donee that he essentially allowed the donee to take control, the plaintiff will have a much better chance of having the donee assume the burden.

Certain states resolve gift presumptions, and their relationship to constructive or resulting trusts, in statutes. Therefore, a careful practitioner needs to not only learn case law but check the statutes on the topic as well. One also has to research how the statutes are interpreted. For example, in Georgia, if property is transferred to a "husband and wife, parent and child, or siblings, a gift shall be presumed, but such presumption shall be rebuttable

---

11. Kurtz v. Kurtz, 144 A.D.2d 468 (N.Y. App. Div. 1988); Laurenzano v. Laurenzano, 156 A.D.2d 430 (N.Y. App. Div. 1989).

12. *See* Matter of Zirinsky, 43 A.D.3d 946 (N.Y. App. Div 2007); Matter of Swain, 125 A.D.2d 574, 575 (N.Y. App. Div. 1986); Patterson v. Patterson, 167 W. Va. 1, 11 (W. Va. 1981).

by clear and convincing evidence."[13] However, one court ruled that this presumption only applied in the context of resulting trusts, and not to constructive trusts, because the statute defining constructive trusts did not mention a familial gift presumption.[14]

One Ohio case had its own way of resolving burden issues. In that case, a late mother had allegedly provided funds to her daughter. The estate sought, among other relief, to impose a constructive trust. If the mother and daughter had a fiduciary relationship, then the daughter would have had the obligation, by clear and convincing evidence, to prove that there really was a gift. However, the court held that a mere familial relationship between a mother and daughter does not mean there is a fiduciary relationship. Therefore, in that case there was a family-gift presumption. As an aside, the court also indicated in dicta that "[i]n the case of a gift from a child to a parent undue influence may be inferred from the relation of the parties, but never where the gift is from the parent to the child."[15]

In other contexts, courts hold that a confidential relationship exists between spouses,[16] a parent and child,[17] siblings,[18] and between a grandparent and grandchild.[19]

---

13. Ga. Code § 53-12-131(c).

14. Roberts v. Smith, 801 S.E.2d 915, 920–21 (Ga. Ct. App. 2017).

15. *In re* Estate of Workman, 2008 Ohio 3351 (Ohio Ct. App. 2008) (citation omitted).

16. *See Foreman v. Foreman*, 251 N.Y. 237, 242 (N.Y. 1929).

17. *See Squiciarino v. Squiciarino*, 35 A.D.3d 844, 845 (N.Y. App. Div. 2006).

18. *See McNeill v. Mohammad*, 32 A.D.3d 829, 830 (N.Y. App. Div. 2006).

19. *See Thaw v. Thaw*, 27 F.2d 729, 731 (2d Cir. 1928).

One court has said that "where a young member of the family is also in a confidential relationship, either of business or advisor, a gift from an older member of the family is presumptively invalid."[20]

Not all property transfers between family members are equal. Some are more equal than others. Some courts have indicated that the "presumption [of a gift] is strongest when the grantee is the wife of the payor or a minor child[,] . . . less strong in the case of an adult son and weaker when a daughter-in-law is involved."[21] Other courts hold that a transfer of property even between a father-in-law and son-in-law is presumed a gift.[22] Other courts hold that the presumption of a gift does not apply between siblings.[23] An attorney has to become familiar with the relevant state law on presumptions for the particular relationship at issue.

A resulting trust is a close sibling to a constructive trust, but resulting trusts sometimes have some critically different (if not confusing) laws concerning the burden. As a reminder, a resulting trust is one in which the grantor pays for the property, has the title put in someone else's name, but still claims it belongs to himself. As Maryland's high court put it,

> It is one of the fundamental principles of equity that where property is purchased, and the legal

20. *Id.* at 733.

21. Chamberlin v. Chamberlin, 116 N.H. 368, 371 (1976) (citations omitted).

22. Somer v. Bogart, 749 S.W.2d 202 (Tex. Ct. App. 1988).

23. *In re* Marriage of Awan, 388 Ill. App. 3d 204, 213 (Ill. App. Ct. 2009).

> title is taken in the name of one person, while the purchase price is paid by another, but not as a loan to the grantee, nor from any natural or moral obligation to provide for the grantee, a resulting trust arises by implication of law in favor of the person paying the purchase price, unless a different intention is shown.[24]

The party seeking to enforce a resulting trust, meaning the one seeking the property, must meet a clear and convincing burden in order to claim an interest in it, at least in some states.[25] That means, at the very least, the donor must prove that he or she paid the purchase price for the property at issue. But that rule about the burden contains qualifications; many presumptions are in favor of the one who put up the funds. Confusingly, the presumption concept and the burden of proof concept, to some degree, do not correlate in lockstep.

In many states, once a party proves he used his own money to purchase property for a nonfamily member, there is a presumption that he has a resulting trust in his own favor. However, if he does the same thing for a close family member, especially if he buys a house, the presumption switches. In that case, it is presumed to be a gift, and there is no longer any presumption of a resulting trust. This is especially the case if the party providing the funds had a legal obligation to provide for the

24. Fasman v. Pottashnick, 188 Md. 105, 109 (1947).

25. Lee v. Lee, 260 Ga. 356, 357 (1990); Gifford v. Dennis, 335 S.E.2d 371, 373 (Va. 1985).

recipient.[26] One Texas court cited the Restatement of the Law of Trusts (Second) section 442 on this issue:

> Where a transfer of property is made by one person and the purchase price is paid by another and the transferee is a wife, child or other natural object of bounty of the person by whom the purchase price is paid, a resulting trust does not arise unless the latter manifests an intention that the transferee should not have the beneficial interest in the property.[27]

For the donor trying to recover property from a family member, there are a few tricks one can use. One could argue that the transferee was not a "natural object of bounty." Or if there is a presumption of a gift, it may be rebutted by proving a different intention of the donor. This is because "unlike a constructive trust, a resulting trust pivots on the key element of intention."[28]

Not only case law but also statutes sometimes delineate the burdens for aspects of a resulting trust case. For example, there is at least one statute that indicates that the person paying the sums is presumed to have the resulting trust, without apparently the obligation to present clear and convincing evidence. In Minnesota, a statute indicates, "If a transfer of property is made to one person and the purchase price is paid by another, a

26. *See* Lollis v. Lollis, 291 S.C. 525, 528–29 (S.C. 1987); Parks v. Zions First Nat'l Bank, 673 P.2d 590, 598 (Utah 1983).

27. Somer v. Bogart, 749 S.W.2d 202, 204 (Tex. App. 1988).

28. Maffei v. Roman Catholic, 449 Mass. 235, 253 (2007).

resulting trust is presumed to arise in favor of the person by whom the purchase price is paid."[29] Montana also has a relevant statute: "When a transfer of property is made to one person and the purchase price is paid by another, a resulting trust arises in favor of the person who paid the purchase price."[30] Even if one's state does not have a statute at issue, case law or references to the Restatement of Law, Trusts, can be helpful to an attorney seeking to litigate such a case.

Not every state follows the same standard. Kansas abolished the common law presumption described earlier by statute: "[w]hen a conveyance for a valuable consideration is made to one person and the consideration therefor paid by another, no . . . trust shall result . . . subject to the provisions of the next two sections."[31] In Kansas, one claiming to be a beneficiary has to prove that an exception to that statute applies, such as that the person receiving the property had an agreement to hold the land in trust for the party paying for it.[32]

Resulting trust law goes through changes just as society changes. For example, in the past, in North Carolina, if a husband provided funds to purchase real estate, and the title was put in his wife's name, it would be presumed to be a gift. But the converse was not true; if a wife had provided the funds for land, but the real property was put in the husband's name, the court would presume there was a resulting trust, and that the wife would be the true

29. MN Stat. § 501B.07 (2013).
30. Mont. Code Ann. § 72-38-122(1).
31. K.S.A. 58-2406.
32. *Id.* 58-2408.

owner. There would be no presumption she would have intended a gift. In the early 1980s, North Carolina ruled for sexual equality, and determined that in either case, the presumption would be it would be a gift, unless the donor provided clear and convincing evidence to rebut that standard.[33] (Therefore, if your client is a rich wife who provided the funds for the real estate, but put it in the husband's name, and then wants her property "back," she will have to hope to face a judge who is old fashioned.)

There are a few other issues with burdens in a resulting trust case. For example, in at least one state, if a contributor only provides a general contribution to the purchase price, and not the entire sum, no resulting trust arises unless it is proven by clear and convincing evidence that it was the contributor's intention, at the time of conveyance, to correspond that partial payment with a beneficial ownership of the whole or some "definite fractional part" of the subject property.[34] Other states have different presumptions. In Maryland,

> where a transfer of property is made to one person, and only a part of the purchase price is paid by another, a resulting trust arises in favor of the person by whom such payment is made in such proportion as the part paid by him bears to the total purchase price, unless he manifests an intention that no resulting trust should arise or that a resulting trust to that extent should not arise.[35]

---

33. Mims v. Mims, 305 N.C. 41, 47 (1982).
34. Cutroneo v. Cutroneo, 81 R.I. 55, 59 (1953).
35. Sines v. Shipes, 192 Md. 139, 153 (1949).

On a separate topic, in New York, there is a presumption that a person who pays money for property, but puts it in another person's name, is doing so in fraud of his then-existing creditors. Therefore, the creditors can use a trust theory to claim a right to that property, unless that presumption is rebutted.[36]

If this were not confusing enough, there seems to be another rule about burdens entirely if the payor purchased the property and put it in his own name and another person jointly. In Florida, a court held that this "is an indication of an intention of the payor to make a beneficial gift of an undivided interest in the property to the other person; and in the absence of evidence of a different intention of the payor, the other person does not hold his interest upon a resulting trust for the payor. This is true whether the transfer was made to the payor and the other person as joint tenants or tenants in common."[37]

Another critical issue is whether the clear and convincing burden would apply only at the trial stage, or whether it would apply at a summary judgment motion stage too. At least one federal court held that in the context of a resulting trust case, a party with the heightened burden to prove a fact with clear and convincing evidence must satisfy that burden in order to survive a

---

36. *See* New York's EPTL § 7-1.3; Hotung v. Cosmopolitan Prop. Sec. Ltd., 2008 N.Y. Slip Op. 32112, 11 (N.Y. Sup. Ct. 2008).

37. Fernandez v. Marrero, 282 So. 3d 928, 931 (Fla. Dist. Ct. App. 2019) (citing cmt. e to section 440 of the Restatement (Second) of Trusts.)

motion for summary judgment.[38] Presumably, that means that the court would have to rule that if the potential evidence presented at the summary judgment motion were believed, it would meet the clear and convincing standard.

B. Evidentiary Issues

1. Parol Evidence

Another one of the benefits of a constructive trust case is that the plaintiff may generally use parol evidence to support his case. Parol evidence is defined as "evidence given orally."[39]

One court gave a good general description of the parol evidence rule:

> Where the parties, without any fraud or mistake, have deliberately put their engagements in writing, the law declares the writing to be not only the best, but the only, evidence of their agreement. All preliminary negotiations, conversations and verbal agreements are merged in and superseded by the subsequent written contract . . . and unless fraud, accident or mistake be averred, the writing constitutes the agreement between the parties, and its terms and agreements cannot be added to nor subtracted from by parol evidence.[40]

38. Guerra v. Abuaita, No. 1:19-cv-01073-STA-jay, at *15 (W.D. Tenn. July 29, 2020).

39. Instone Travel Tech Marine v. Intern. Shipping, 334 F.3d 423, 432 (5th Cir. 2003), citing Black's Law Dictionary 579 (7th ed. 1999).

40. Gianni v. Russell Co., 281 Pa. 320, 323 (Pa. 1924) (citation omitted).

In the context of a constructive trust case, the parol evidence rule would generally be a non sequitur. After all, most constructive trust cases do not concern written contracts or an attempt to avoid the effects of a written contract. In addition, constructive trust cases often do include fraud, accidents, or mistake, which would be another basis for using parol evidence even if there were a contract. Also the rule does not even prohibit a party from introducing parol evidence to prove fraudulent inducement.[41]

Most case law on constructive trusts confirms that parol evidence is permissible evidence in the context of a constructive trust case. "Since a constructive trust is found for the purpose of preventing humans from being successful in shady bits of behavior, it is universally recognized that the required operative facts can be proved by parol."[42] A constructive trust "arises by implication from the relationship and conduct of the parties and may be established by parol testimony."[43] Some courts also indicate that because the statute of frauds is no defense to a constructive trust case, then under the same rationale, a plaintiff seeking a constructive trust may use parol evidence to prove his case.[44]

Regardless, some courts do not accept parol evidence with open arms. That is in part because there is such a

---

41. Galmish v. Cicchini, 90 Ohio St. 3d 22, 28 (Ohio 2000).

42. Hertz v. Klavan, 374 A.2d 871, 873 (D.C. 1977) (citation omitted).

43. Allgood v. Allgood, 473 So. 2d 416, 421 (Miss. 1985).

44. *See, e.g.*, Ubriaco v. Martino, 36 A.D.3d 793, 794 (N.Y. App. Div. 2007) (citation omitted).

heavy burden necessary to prove a constructive trust. At least one court held that it viewed parol testimony about a constructive trust "with caution."[45]

One potentially critical issue is whether the parol evidence at issue addresses real property ownership, and whether the deed already appears to resolve that issue. For example, in one case there was a challenge concerning whether the named parties on a deed were the actual owners, or whether there was a constructive trust implicitly indicating that only one was the owner. The court held that the deed itself was a "contract in writing" and therefore the parties could not use parol evidence to establish an oral constructive trust on the real property.[46] (Surprisingly, the same court in that case held that the parol evidence rule does not bar evidence proving the existence of a resulting trust.)

Other courts see it differently. For example, one court rejected an argument that parol evidence is inadmissible to invalidate a deed. This was because "establishment of a constructive trust does not contemplate the setting aside of the deeds. To the contrary, it proceeds on the theory that, even though the legal title rests in the grantee of the deed, equity will declare that such title is held in trust for someone else to whom it rightfully belongs."[47] A litigator facing an issue about a deed will have to scour his or her own state's case law to find the best answer for the client.

---

45. Barriffe v. Estate of Nelson, 153 So. 3d 613, 618 (Miss. 2014).

46. *In re* Bullard, No. 02-52968, Ad. Proc. No. 034106, at *3 (Bankr. M.D.N.C. July 2, 2004).

47. Borsgard v. Elverum, 248 Minn. 405, 412 (1957).

C. The Dead Man's Statute

As many constructive trust cases concern actions of an already dead person, and what that person's wishes were, the so-called dead man's statute may become a critical issue.

The dead man's statute does not exist in every state, but a well-known version was enacted by New York's legislature decades ago. Its statute, CPLR 4519, disqualifies parties interested in litigation from testifying about personal transactions or communications with deceased or mentally ill persons. The purpose of the rule is to protect the estate of the deceased from claims of the living who, through their own perjury, could make factual assertions that the decedent could not refute in court.[48]

There are of course exceptions to the statute. For example, if the representative of the deceased introduces the testimony of the decedent into evidence at trial, then the representative has opened the door to such testimony.

Reviewing certain cases is helpful to understand how the dead man's statute works in a constructive trust case. The Supreme Court of Alabama had two cases on the subject. In *Walling v. Couch*,[49] a husband conveyed real estate to his wife (deceased) with the understanding that she would build a house on the property, and if the property were ever sold, the husband would receive back the value of the property. They subsequently divorced and she sold the property to third parties. The husband sued

---

48. Sepulveda v. Aviles, 308 A.D.2d 1, 10 (N.Y. App. Div. 2003).
49. 292 Ala. 33 (1973).

the estate and third parties alleging constructive trust. The court held that the dead man's statute rendered incompetent all testimony concerning conversations between the husband and his deceased wife respecting the alleged agreement.

In contradistinction is another Supreme Court of Alabama case, *Finch v. York*,[50] where a father (deceased) conveyed real estate to a son and a daughter with the alleged agreement that they would reconvey a one-half interest to two other daughters not then present. The son declined to make the conveyance, and was alleged to hold the property in trust. The court distinguished *Walling* and held that evidence of statements made by the deceased father were admissible under the Alabama dead man's statute because the estate would be neither increased nor decreased as a result of the suit.

Not all dead man's statutes are born alike. For example, one critical issue for Washington D.C.'s statute is whether the testimony on the subject is uncorroborated. In one of its interesting constructive trust cases,[51] a mother and daughter put their name on a deed as joint tenants, and when the mother died, the daughter was the sole owner of record. The daughter's siblings claimed a constructive trust, arguing that they had all contributed to the purchase and maintenance of the home, and that the deed of record was prepared as a matter of convenience, and not that the mother intended to deprive the rest of the family of the house. Therefore, some of the

50. 294 Ala. 382 (1975).

51. Gray v. Gray, 412 A.2d 1208 (D.C. 1980).

critical issues could have been the late mother's communications with the family about the home.

The daughter lost the case, and then on appeal claimed that all of the plaintiffs' testimony about the transactions with, or actions, declarations, or admissions of their late mother should have been barred under the dead man's statute. But the court held that the statute was intended to protect a person representing the deceased against potentially fraudulent suits based only on a claimant's word that the deceased was under an obligation to the claimant. The court held that a claimant's testimony is sufficient, however, if corroborating evidence, taken as a whole, tends to make his or her position substantially more credible. In that case, some of the corroborating evidence came from the record title holding daughter herself; she was unable to explain why only her name was on the deed. Another piece of corroborating evidence was that the record title holding daughter had written a letter to her brother stating that "Mama wanted the house to be kept so that the children will have a place to stay if they wanted to live there."[52] The record title holder's brothers and sisters also produced checks and receipts indicating payments by children (other than that daughter) on the home loan, carrying charges, and other household expenses. Therefore, the court held that the dead man's statute did not warrant reversal of the judgment.

52. Lesson—never write letters to family members.

D. Hearsay Evidence

Hearsay can come up in nearly any lawsuit. In a constructive trust one example might concern oral promises. If a party were to try to claim that oral promise was inadmissible hearsay, that claim should fail. That is because one introduces that evidence not to prove a fact but rather to prove that the parties engaged in a verbal action. As one court put it, "The hearsay rule does not exclude relevant testimony as to what the contracting parties said with respect to the making or the terms of an oral agreement."[53] On a related topic, if a party wishes to introduce a statement that someone made about their intent in transferring property, even it were hearsay, it should be admissible under the state of mind exception to the hearsay rule, as a declaration of intent.[54]

E. Bench Trials versus Jury Trials

In the unlikely case that a constructive trust case ever winds up in a trial, one critical matter to resolve is whether it should be heard and resolved by a judge or by a jury. This depends in part in how complicated the issues are, and which way the emotional issues might hit a jury.

Since the underlying case is for equitable relief, one has to keep in mind that the ultimate decision cannot

---

53. State of N.Y. v. Hendrickson Bros., Inc., 840 F.2d 1065, 1075 (2d Cir. 1988) (citation omitted).

54. *See* FED. R. EVID. 803 (3); Clooney v. Clooney, 118 N.H. 754, 756 (1978).

be resolved by a jury. But that's not the end to the question. In a case concerning equitable relief similar to a constructive trust, a Texas court noted that a "jury does not determine the expediency, necessity, or propriety of equitable relief. . . . However, when contested fact issues must be resolved before equitable relief can be determined, a party is entitled to have that resolution made by a jury."[55]

This concept can be very helpful to a defendant who has committed acts that a typical person off the street might consider reprehensible. Although a jury might be ready to lynch a defendant who had tricked an old lady out of her property, in theory a judge might have a more measured approach, and even decide that a constructive trust was not an appropriate remedy.

When a jury is resolving part of a case concerning a constructive trust, and the judge another part, there can be some tricky issues. For example, in the Oregon case *Evergreen West Business Center, LLC v. Emmert*,[56] the plaintiff was a limited liability company that had a defendant, who was one of its members, save its property from foreclosure by a lender. Defendant saved the property from foreclosure in his own selfish way—by purchasing the loan and associated encumbrance for his own benefit for $613,979.49. Defendant then foreclosed on the property himself, bought it at a foreclosure sale, and then encumbered the property with a $900,000 loan from a different lender. The plaintiff sought both monetary damages and

---

55. Burrow v. Arce, 997 S.W.2d 229, 245 (Tex. 1999) (citations and internal quotation marks omitted).

56. 323 P.3d 250, 252 (Or. 2014).

for a constructive trust–the sale of the premises with the proceeds split up among the members, instead of just the defendant. In that case, the jury awarded money damages of lost profit of only $1, and punitive damages of $600,000.

When the defendant moved to reduce the punitive damages, the court reduced them to only $4, which made the entire damages a grand total of $5—just barely enough to buy a movie ticket in the Stone Age.[57] Then the judge made an offer to plaintiff—to keep the $5, or to obtain a constructive trust. Without too much surprise, the plaintiff chose the constructive trust. The particular result from that trust was a creative but logical one—that the property would go to the plaintiff, it would then be sold, and from the proceeds, the plaintiff would repay defendant the $613,979.49 (that defendant originally paid.) And the defendant in essence would have to use those funds to pay off the new loan he encumbered it with.

When the case was argued before the intermediate appellate level court, the defendant argued that the jury's verdict determined that the "unjust benefit" to defendant was $1 and, for that reason, the trial court lacked authority to impose a constructive trust that would allow plaintiff to recover more than that amount. That court agreed. However, the state Supreme Court agreed with the original trial court.

The Oregon Supreme Court held that "the jury's damage finding did not foreclose equitable relief because the trial court did not adopt it, and that finding was not necessary to plaintiff's constructive trust claim. Nor was

---

57. Meaning when I was in high school.

the constructive trust remedy identical to the damage award because plaintiff sought a sale of the disputed property. And, finally, plaintiff—not defendant—was entitled to elect its preferred remedy before the entry of final judgment."[58]

The Supreme Court noted that there was a difference between the jury's function and the judge's function. The court also noted that there was a difference between the concept of the actual money damages versus the equitable relief that could make one whole in a different manner. The court held that

> the jury's damage finding was based on its determination of the value of the property when defendant acquired it at the foreclosure sale. In contrast, in the constructive trust claim, plaintiff sought specific relief that did not require a determination of the value of the property at that point in time. Instead, that relief assigned to plaintiff the potential benefit—as well as the risk of loss—associated with holding the property for a court-ordered sale that would facilitate the winding-up of plaintiff's affairs and satisfaction of its debts. . . . [P]laintiff was entitled to pursue that relief, even though the jury had determined that plaintiff's actual money damages were a mere dollar. Because the constructive trust claim focused on a different sort of unjust enrichment—that is, the benefit of owning the property itself—the jury's

58. *Id.* at 260.

> damage finding was not material to the availability of equitable relief.[59]

That kind of case reveals that a plaintiff should always make sure to keep a constructive trust argument in its back pocket. Perhaps a realist's way of looking at that case is that the judge believed the jury was wrong, and simply wanted to look for an excuse to provide appropriate relief to the plaintiff. That is certainly what the defendant, in essence, argued. But the moral of the story is that constructive trusts can be an invaluable tool to protect a plaintiff from a fiduciary, even if (1) traditional damages would not provide full relief, (2) one believes a jury would not be sophisticated enough to understand the instructions given to them, or even (3) one believes that a jury may have its own irrational reasons for not wishing to award appropriate damages to the plaintiff.

A case on a related issue, which went the other way, reveals the potential dangers of leaving critical facts to be resolved by a jury, because they may prevent the judge from issuing a constructive trust even if the court wishes to do so. In the case *Brown v. F.S.L.I.C*,[60] the jury awarded some damages but also returned special verdicts in which it found specifically that certain defendants did not commit intentional fraud, negligent misrepresentation, or conspiracy. Regardless, the trial court awarded a constructive trust over additional funds, on the concept that those defendants had imputed knowledge of improprieties, and that they were not bona fide purchasers

59. *Id.* at 258.
60. 105 Nev. 409 (1989).

without knowledge. (As indicated elsewhere in this book, bona fide purchasers cannot be held liable for a constructive trust.) The Supreme Court of Nevada reversed, and vacated the constructive trust relief. It held that the jury's verdict implicitly rejected all the plaintiff's theories of imputed knowledge. Therefore, when the trial court granted constructive trust relief, it had violated the rule that when deciding whether to grant equitable relief, the court is prohibited from reconsidering any issues necessarily and actually decided by the jury.

If any reader has miraculously made it to the end of this book, I congratulate you, and wish you the best of luck in any constructive trust litigation.

Appendix A
Sample Complaints

The following are various sample portions of complaints that may be of some use in planning out how to plead a potential case in which one seeks constructive trust relief, or related relief. Of course, one must be fully familiar with the local law to determine how to prepare complaints and what elements are necessary to allege a prima facie case.

Sample Complaint 1

Plaintiff, by his attorneys, ________, complaining of the defendants, alleges as follows:

1. Plaintiff ____, is a natural person residing at ____.
2. Defendant ____ is a natural person residing at ____.
3. Defendant ____ is a natural person residing at ____.
4. The defendants' actions described in this complaint took place at ____.
5. This complaint seeks relief based on real property allegedly owned by defendants.

6. On or about ____, plaintiff became the owner of the premises known as known as ____ ("Premises"), pursuant to a recorded deed.
7. The Premises are located in Block ____, Lot ____ of the County of ____. The following is a description of the Premises:

   All that certain plot, piece or parcel of land, with the buildings and improvements thereon erected, situate, lying and being in the Borough of ____.

AS AND FOR A FIRST CAUSE OF ACTION

8. Plaintiff seeks relief under Article 15 of the Real Property Actions and Proceedings Law, to clear a cloud upon title, as well as under Real Property Law 329, to cancel an instrument of record.
9. On or about 20xx, a certain deed ("20xx Deed") concerning the Premises was allegedly executed to the benefit of defendant ____.
10. The 20xx Deed was subsequently recorded at CRFN (City Register File Number). . . .
11. Defendants obtained plaintiff's signature on the 20xx deed through subterfuge, and intentionally misinformed plaintiff about the nature of the document, making those statements with knowledge of their falsity, with the intent to deceive plaintiff.
12. Plaintiff and defendants have a confidential and fiduciary relationship.
13. Plaintiff is the father of both defendants.
14. Defendants informed plaintiff, at ____ location, on or around the time when he was asked to execute the

20xx deed, that the 20xx deed indicated that even after executing it, plaintiff would still be either the sole owner of the premises, or that estate would continue to be an owner of the Premises after his death.

15. Plaintiff reasonably relied on the misrepresentations made by Defendants.
16. Defendants committed fraud against Plaintiff.
17. It appears that defendants claim, or it appears from the public records that the defendants might claim an interest in the Premises, due to the fact that they have a recorded deed concerning the Premises.
18. Defendants' claims are unjust and the plaintiff stands seized and possessed the Premises free of and wholly discharged from any and every such claim or lien by defendant.
19. None of the defendants are unknown and none are infants, or incompetent to manage themselves or their affairs, or mentally retarded,[1] mentally ill, or an alcohol abuser.
20. Any judgment granted herein will not affect any person or persons not in being or ascertained at the commencement of this action, who by any contingence contained in a devise or grant or otherwise could afterward become entitled to a beneficial estate or interest in the Premises, and that every person in being who would have been entitled to such estate or interest, if such event had happened immediately before the commencement of the action, is named as a party herein.

---

1. N.Y. RPAPL 1515 contains this language, even though portions may not seem politically correct speech.

21. By reason of the foregoing, plaintiff is entitled to a declaratory judgment declaring the 20xx Deed void, vacated, and set aside, and for such other and further relief as may to the court seem proper.
22. Defendants' undue influence and/or fraud against plaintiff continued from the date of the alleged transfer to present.
23. By reason of the foregoing, the plaintiff is entitled to declaratory judgment that he is the sole owner of the Premises.
24. In the alternative, the plaintiff is entitled to declaratory judgment that the 20xx Deed should be deemed null and void, and stricken from the records.
25. By reason of the foregoing, alternatively the plaintiff is entitled to specific performance, and an order requiring the defendants to transfer to Premises to plaintiff.

AS AND FOR A SECOND CAUSE OF ACTION

26. In the alternative to the above cause of action, there is a cause of action based on unilateral or mutual mistake.
27. Before the 20xx Deed was drafted, all parties had informed the drafter to prepare it in such a manner so as to indicate that plaintiff would remain a partial owner of the premises, as a tenant in common.
28. Plaintiff sought to remain a partial owner of the premises, as a tenant in common, in part to ensure that ____ would be permitted to remain in the premises after plaintiff's death.
29. Before the 20xx Deed was drafted, all parties had informed the drafter to prepare it in such a manner so as to indicate that ____ would not be an owner of the premises.

30. After the 20xx deed was drafted, plaintiff had believed that its contents indicated that he was to remain a partial owner of the Premises as at least a tenant in common, and not a simple life estate holder.
31. After the 20xx Deed was drafted, plaintiff had believed that ____ would not be deemed a partial owner of the Premises pursuant to that deed.
32. After the 20xx Deed was drafted, defendants had believed that its contents indicated that plaintiff was to remain a partial owner of the Premises, and that defendant ____ would not be deemed a partial owner of the Premises pursuant to that deed.
33. Plaintiff executed the 20xx Deed based on his reasonable belief that its terms indicated that he would remain a partial owner of the Premises, as a tenant in common (and not simply a life estate holder) and that ____ would not be a partial owner.
34. However, after the 20xx Deed was drafted and executed, all parties discovered that pursuant to its terms, plaintiff retained only a life estate to the Premises, and that the deed mistakenly failed to indicate plaintiff retained an ownership interest as a common tenant.
35. In addition, after the 20xx Deed was drafted and executed, all parties discovered that pursuant to its terms, defendant ____ was described as a partial owner of the premises.
36. By reason of the foregoing, plaintiff is entitled to a declaratory judgment declaring the 20xx Deed void, vacated, and set aside, and for such other and further relief as may to the court seem proper.
37. By reason of the foregoing, the plaintiff is entitled to declaratory judgment that he is the sole owner of the Premises.

38. By reason of the foregoing, alternatively the plaintiff is entitled to specific performance, and an order requiring the defendants to transfer full ownership of the Premises to plaintiff.
39. In the alternative, the plaintiff is entitled to declaratory judgment that the 20xx Deed should be deemed null and void, and stricken from the records.
40. In the alternative, the plaintiff is entitled to declaratory judgment that the 20xx Deed be reformed to indicate he is at least a partial owner as a common tenant of the Premises with ____, as well as a life estate holder, and that ____ should not be deemed a partial owner, and for related relief including injunctive relief in order to allow plaintiff to have such rights.

AS AND FOR A THIRD CAUSE OF ACTION

41. Plaintiff seeks a constructive trust based on the following claims.
42. Plaintiff and defendants have a confidential and fiduciary relationship.
43. Plaintiff is the father of both defendants.
44. At the time plaintiff executed the 20xx Deed, the defendants made a promise to transfer the Premises to plaintiff upon his request.
45. Alternatively, at the time plaintiff executed the 20xx Deed, the defendants made a promise to transfer a partial interest to the Premises to plaintiff upon his request.
46. Plaintiff relied on the defendants' promise, when he executed the 20xx Deed.
47. Defendants provided no consideration to plaintiff in return for the 20xx Deed.

48. At this time plaintiff executed the 20xx Deed, defendants agreed and understood that plaintiff wished to retain an ownership interest in the Premises, and not solely as a life estate holder.
49. Defendants have been unjustly enriched from the alleged transfer of the Premises to them.
50. Plaintiff has requested that defendants transfer a full interest in the premises to the plaintiff.
51. In the alternative, plaintiff has requested that defendants transfer a partial interest in the premises to the plaintiff.
52. Defendants previously indicated that they would consent to transferring a full ownership interest in the premises to the plaintiff.
53. In the alternative, defendants previously indicated that they would consent to transferring a partial ownership interest in the premises to the plaintiff.
54. Less than _____ years before this action was filed, defendants first informed plaintiff that they would not transfer any interest in the Premises to plaintiff.
55. No adequate remedy exists at law. Money damages would be inadequate to compensate the plaintiff including without limitation due to the fact that the underlying issues concern unique real property.
56. Even in the event that defendants had not made a promise to the plaintiff, the defendants acquired the Premises in such circumstances that they cannot in good conscience retain the interest.
57. Plaintiff is entitled to an equitable and constructive trust on the Premises.
58. By reason of the foregoing, plaintiff is entitled to a declaratory judgment declaring the 20xx Deed void, vacated, and set aside, and for such other and further relief as may to the court seem proper.

59. By reason of the foregoing, the plaintiff is entitled to declaratory judgment that he is the sole owner of the Premises.
60. By reason of the foregoing, alternatively the plaintiff is entitled to specific performance, and an order requiring the defendants to transfer to Premises to plaintiff.
61. In the alternative, the plaintiff is entitled to declaratory judgment that he is at least a partial owner of the Premises, and that the defendants shall transfer partial ownership to the plaintiff, as a tenant in common.

AS AND FOR A FOURTH CAUSE OF ACTION

62. Plaintiff has spent monies on the Premises, including for real estate taxes, mortgage, insurance, repairs, utilities, and maintenance.
63. Defendants have refused to repay plaintiff for the sums of monies he has invested into the Premises. These sums included, without limitations, both the monies he invested to purchase the premises, and the monies he used to pay off the mortgage, both after and before the 20xx Deed was executed.
64. Defendants would be unjustly enriched if they were permitted to retain the value of the sums plaintiff invested into the Premises, including without limitation the initial purchase by plaintiff.
65. Defendants would be unjustly enriched if they were permitted to retain the Premises, as they provided no sums to purchase the premises or to pay for any of the costs of the premises.
66. As a result, plaintiff has been damaged in the amount of at least $____.

AS AND FOR A FIFTH CAUSE OF ACTION

67. Plaintiff transferred ownership interest to defendants due to their undue influence against him.
68. When plaintiff transferred an ownership interest to defendants, it was an unconscionable transfer of his interests.
69. The influence exercised by defendants amounted to a moral coercion, which restrained independent action and destroyed free agency, or which, by importunity which could not be resisted, and constrained the plaintiff to do that which was against his free will and desire, but which he was unable to refuse or too weak to resist.
70. Defendants' continuing nature of their undue influence against plaintiff tolled any statute of limitation period.
71. Defendants' undue influence against plaintiff continued from the date of the alleged transfer to present.
72. By reason of the foregoing, alternatively the plaintiff is entitled to specific performance, and an order requiring the defendants to transfer to Premises to plaintiff.
73. In the alternative, the plaintiff is entitled to declaratory judgment that he is at least a partial owner of the Premises, and that the defendants shall transfer partial ownership to the plaintiff, as a tenant in common.
74. In the alternative, the plaintiff is entitled to declaratory judgment that the 20xx Deed should be deemed null and void, and stricken from the records.

AS AND FOR A SIXTH CAUSE OF ACTION

75. Defendants indicated in a signed letter dated ____ that they intended to allow plaintiff to be named as partial owner of the premises.
76. This letter constituted an enforceable agreement.
77. Defendants have breached the terms of this agreement.
78. Plaintiff is entitled to specific performance, requiring defendants to execute a deed naming him as partial owner of the premises. In the alternative, plaintiff is entitled to money damages based in part on the costs plaintiff incurred with respect to the premises, which he incurred in reliance, in part, on this letter.

Wherefore, plaintiff demands judgment against the defendant as follows:

(a) On his first, second, third, and fifth causes of action, a declaratory judgment declaring the 20xx Deed as void, vacated, and set aside, a declaratory judgment that he is the sole owner of the Premises, and an order requiring the defendants to transfer to Premises to plaintiff, or alternatively for an order that plaintiff is, in addition to a life estate holder, also a common tenant and partial owner of the Premises.
(b) On his fourth cause of action, damages in the sum of $1,000,000;
(c) On his sixth cause of action, specific performance and damages in the sum of $1,000,000;
(d) for such other and further relief as this court deems just and proper.

Sample Complaint 2

Plaintiff, by his attorneys, ____, complaining of the defendants, alleges as follows:

1. Plaintiff ____ is an individual doing business in ____.
2. Plaintiff XYZ Co. is a corporation doing business in ____.
3. Mrs. X is an individual living in ____.
4. Mr. X died on ____; he killed himself.
5. Mrs. X was the wife, and now widow of Mr. X.
6. Plaintiffs had hired the late Mr. X to operate plaintiffs' business in ____ as follows ____.
7. The late Mr. X illegally and improperly drafted $____ in checks from one or more of plaintiffs' accounts without plaintiffs receiving anything in return.
8. The late Mr. X illegally and improperly removed at least $____ in cash from one or more of plaintiffs' accounts without plaintiffs receiving anything in return.
9. The late Mr. X used the checks and cash to purchase, repair, or improve real estate located at ____, which was owned by Mr. and Mrs. X.
10. The late Mr. X used the checks and cash to purchase life insurance policies, the proceeds of which would be in favor of defendant Mrs. X.

AS AND FOR A FIRST CAUSE OF ACTION FOR INTENTIONAL MISREPRESENTATION, FRAUD, AND CONVERSION

11. On or about ____, the late Mr. X induced plaintiffs to hire Mr. X by representing he could be trusted to act in the best interest of plaintiffs and that he would not take funds of plaintiffs. He made those statements

at ____ location. These statements were intended to induce plaintiffs to rely on his representations.

12. Since ____, the late Mr. X continued to represent to plaintiffs that he was acting in the best interests of plaintiffs, and was rendering honest accountings.
13. These statements were intended to induce plaintiffs to rely on his representations.
14. The plaintiffs reasonably relied on his representations, and allowed him to continue to be employed for plaintiffs, and allowed Mr. X to have access to plaintiffs' banking and checking accounts.
15. During the same time, Mr. X concealed the fact that his representations were false and that he was taking and using checks and cash of plaintiffs for his own purposes.
16. Mr. X had a position of trust and confidence toward plaintiffs, and a fiduciary duty toward them.
17. Mr. X converted plaintiffs' assets, ultimately transferred them to Mrs. X, used those assets to purchase goods or property for Mrs. X, and/or improved Mrs. X's property.

AS AND FOR A SECOND CAUSE OF ACTION FOR A CONSTRUCTIVE TRUST

18. By virtue of Mr. X's wrongful acts, the insurance proceeds and the real property described above, plus any other real or personal property acquired, improved, maintained, or repaired with the funds described above, are being held by Mrs. X as constructive trustee for the benefit of Plaintiffs.

Sample Complaint 3

Plaintiff, by his attorneys, ________, complaining of the defendants, alleges as follows:

1. Plaintiff "Lender" is an individual doing business in _____
2. Nonparty, the late Brother 1, was the majority shareholder, director, and officer of XYZ, Inc.
3. The late Brother 1 requested a loan from plaintiff in favor of XYZ, Inc.
4. As a material inducement to advance funds to XYZ, Inc., both the late Brother 1 and XYZ, Inc. agreed to maintain a $1 million insurance policy on Brother 1's life for the benefit of Plaintiff.
5. In reliance on that material inducement, plaintiff loaned XYZ, Inc. $1 million.
6. Plaintiff was originally named the beneficiary of the policy, as of 2018.
7. However, on a later date, 2019, Brother 1 submitted a change form to the insurer, naming his Brother 2 as the sole beneficiary of the policy.
8. The change in policy was done without plaintiff's knowledge or authorization.
9. The change in policy was done in order to defeat plaintiff's security interest in the loan it had made to XYZ, Inc.
10. XYZ, Inc. is without the ability to repay the loan.
11. Brother 1 died in 2020.
12. Plaintiff has an equitable interest in the policy proceeds, superior to those of Brother 2.
13. If Brother 2 were allowed to retain the death benefit, he would be unjustly enriched.

14. Money damages would not compensate Plaintiff, in part because XYZ, Inc. has no assets and is no longer doing business.
15. By reason of the foregoing, the court should impose a constructive trust on $____ of the policy's death benefit in favor of Plaintiff.

Sample Complaint 4

1. This case involves the fraudulent diversion of not less than $xxx million from plaintiff to corporate defendants R & D Inc. and S & P Inc., through a former employee of plaintiff named Defendant Z. Upon information and belief, Defendant Z illegally misappropriated and diverted the funds for the benefit of himself.
2. Plaintiff now seeks the return of the money fraudulently conveyed to defendants. The total amount of ill-gotten gains and misappropriated funds received by defendants is $__ million.
3. Following the initial transfer, an overwhelming majority of the proceeds was transferred into several other bank accounts, including personal accounts controlled by Defendant Z.
4. The Plaintiff's businesses at issue in this case finance the acquisition, sale, and leasing of, among other things, widgets. Defendant Z falsely represented to his former colleagues, supervisors and other plaintiff representatives that the corporate defendants were distributors of used widgets. However, the corporate defendants are privately held corporations that do not have any connection to the widget industry.

5. Between approximately 20xx and 20yy, including the following dates and times ____ and at the following locations ____ Defendant Z induced his former employer, plaintiff, to transfer at least $____ million to at least three bank accounts held in the corporate defendants' names. In doing so, Defendant Z made numerous false representations to his colleagues, supervisors, and other plaintiff representatives and provided fabricated documents falsely indicating that the corporate defendants had sold thousands of used widgets to at least four dealers with whom plaintiff had preexisting business relationships.
6. Based on these false statements and actions, and in reasonable reliance on these false statements and actions, plaintiff transferred $__ million in ten separate transactions to the corporate defendants. In fact, these four widget dealers had no relationship whatsoever with the corporate defendants, the dealers had never purchased or attempted to purchase any widgets from the corporate defendants, and the corporate defendants never provided any widgets to the dealers.
7. Within hours of receiving the funds from plaintiff, defendants transferred a substantial amount of the funds out of defendants' bank accounts and into other bank accounts, including personal accounts held by Defendant Z, as part of his further effort to misappropriate the funds. Between approximately 20xx to 20yy, Defendant Z made false oral and written statements to his colleagues, supervisors, and other of plaintiff's representatives in a further effort to conceal the true purpose of the transfers.

8. The misappropriated funds were then used and continue to be used for the benefit of the corporate defendants, and defendant Z. By way of example only and without limitation, plaintiff's funds were used to pay down a $____ million loan that had been procured from a bank where several defendants maintained accounts; plaintiff's funds were transferred to personal accounts held at different banks for Defendant Z, who had signatory and withdrawal authority for both of the corporate defendants' accounts; plaintiff's funds were transferred to at least one personal account held by Defendant Z, who had signatory and withdrawal authority for R & D Inc.'s corporate accounts; plaintiff seeks the return of the funds misappropriated from the plaintiffs.
9. On 20aa, the Court found that plaintiff had demonstrated a substantial likelihood of proving at least one cause of action against the corporate defendants, which would result in the recovery of the misappropriated funds. As a result, the Court entered a temporary restraining order that prohibits the defendants and others from further diverting any of the $xxx million that rightfully belongs to the plaintiff.
10. On information and belief, the temporary restraining order has not frozen all of the funds fraudulently obtained by the defendants. Accordingly, there is a real and imminent risk that defendants will further hide, transfer, or deplete the funds misappropriated from plaintiff by the corporate defendants. Indeed, defendants have already closed various accounts, opened new accounts, and moved the funds multiple times. Accordingly, plaintiff seeks, among other things, a preliminary and permanent injunction

freezing the assets held in defendants' bank accounts at XXX Banks and any accounts into which those funds flowed since 20____, to prevent defendants from further hiding, transferring, depleting or absconding with plaintiff funds. Plaintiff further seeks a writ of attachment over Defendant Z's assets and a preliminary and permanent injunction freezing the assets controlled by Defendant Z to prevent him from further hiding, transferring, depleting, or absconding with plaintiff's funds.

FACTS COMMON TO ALL COUNTS

11. Prior to approximately 20____, X Bank provided inventory financing to dealers that sold widgets, including "Dealer DL," and end users. In connection with financing transactions in the ordinary course of business, plaintiff made wire transfers from time to time to the dealers or end users.
12. Upon information and belief, since at least 20____, Defendant Z solicited and accepted money from plaintiff purportedly to pursue special investment "opportunities." Defendant Z represented to those individuals, agents of plaintiff, that he had access to special investment opportunities. To take advantage of these "opportunities," the individuals wired or wrote personal checks to Defendant Z, who deposited these sums in his personal bank accounts. Defendant Z promised these individuals that they would receive back their initial investment, interest, and a return in six months.
13. Since at least, 20__, the corporate defendants and Defendant Z have conducted a scheme to defraud plaintiff out of millions of dollars and to deprive

plaintiff of Defendant Z's honest services. Defendant Z used at least some of the funds he and the other defendants wrongfully received from plaintiff to pay those individuals who provided Defendant Z with money for the purported investment opportunities he presented.

14. In furtherance of this scheme, defendants prepared or caused to be prepared false transaction documents showing a series of sham sales transactions between the corporate defendants and Dealer DL that never took place. Thereafter, Defendant Z made repeated false statements designed to conceal the fraud. For example, Defendant Z falsely represented to his colleagues, supervisors, and other plaintiff representatives in numerous emails, telephone conversations, and meetings that he had spoken with Dealer DL about these purported transactions, who had provided him with proof that the loan extended by plaintiff had been repaid.
15. In fact, Defendant Z had never spoken with Dealer DL about these purported transactions and never received any such proof because the transactions never occurred.
16. Misled into believing that these sham transactions were legitimate, plaintiff transferred funds to the corporate defendants who had purportedly arranged to provide Dealer DL with thousands of widgets. Plaintiff transferred funds into the following bank accounts over which defendants had signatory and withdrawal authority ____ (collectively, the "defendants' bank accounts").
17. Within hours of the many wire transfers, certain defendants transferred a substantial amount of plaintiff's

funds into other bank accounts, some of which were controlled by Defendant Z. Other amounts were used to pay off a $____ loan procured by R & D. Inc. and taxes owed by at least one defendant.

18. Despite defendants' deception, the scheme was detected, and plaintiff learned that the corporate defendants did not have any relationship whatsoever with Dealer DL. Thus, defendants wrongfully obtained at least $xx million, which was transferred into their bank accounts.
19. If defendants are permitted to retain plaintiff's funds, plaintiff will be irreparably injured, as its legal remedy—a monetary judgment following a full trial—would not be adequate, as the defendants appear to be secreting assets.
20. Defendants are not entitled to the funds, and their continued possession of the funds will irreparably injure plaintiff.

COUNT I: Money Had and Received

21. Defendants wrongly induced plaintiff to transfer, and plaintiff did transfer, at least $xxx of their own funds into defendants' bank accounts, to which defendants were not entitled.
22. Defendants wrongly induced plaintiff to transfer, and plaintiff did transfer, at least $xxx of their own funds into defendants' bank accounts to which defendants were not entitled.
23. Within hours of the wire transfers, defendants transferred a substantial amount of plaintiff's funds into other accounts controlled by Defendant Z, and others.

24. Upon information and belief, defendants wrongfully continue to hold plaintiff's funds in defendants' bank accounts and other accounts controlled by Defendant Z, and others.
25. The funds belong to plaintiff in equity and good conscience.
26. By reason of defendants' actions, plaintiff has been, and will continue to be, seriously and irreparably damaged.
27. Plaintiff has no adequate remedy at law to compensate it for the damage caused by defendants' actions. Accordingly, plaintiff seeks preliminary and permanent injunctive relief enjoining defendants either directly or indirectly, for themselves, or through, on behalf of, or in conjunction with any person, persons, officers, agents, servants, employees, attorneys, or legal entity, from gaining or having access to, transferring, moving, depleting, hiding, pledging, spending, using, or secreting assets in defendants' bank accounts, including safety deposit boxes, or any and all other accounts into which funds from these principal accounts flowed.

COUNT II: Uniform Fraudulent Transfer Act

28. Defendant Z and the corporate defendants, by diverting or transferring the wrongfully obtained funds, engaged in "transfer[s]" within the meaning prescribed in Code # of the Uniform Transfer Act.
29. Defendant Z and the corporate defendants' transfers were made with the actual intent to hinder, delay, or defraud plaintiff and defendants' other creditors, in violation of Uniform Fraudulent Transfer Act.

30. Defendant Z and the corporate defendants' intent to hinder, delay, or defraud is demonstrated by, among other things, the false representations made by Defendant Z to his colleagues, supervisors, and other plaintiff representatives in numerous emails, telephone conversations, and meetings, that the loans extended had been repaid.
31. Defendant Z and the corporate defendants' conduct represents fraudulent transfers under Uniform Fraudulent Transfer Act *et seq.* Plaintiff is entitled to avoid all such transfers, to obtain a writ of attachment against funds in possession of defendants and third parties, to preliminary injunctive relief, and to damages against defendants in an amount to be proven at trial.

COUNT III: Breach of Fiduciary Duty

32. Defendant Z held a position of special trust and confidence with plaintiff. As a result, Defendant Z owed fiduciary duties to plaintiff, including duties of loyalty, care, good faith, and fidelity. Defendant Z also owed fiduciary duties under X state's common law.
33. Defendant Z breached his fiduciary duties to plaintiff by, among other things, knowingly and intentionally appropriating plaintiff funds without the effective and informed consent of plaintiff and with the intent to defraud plaintiff of the funds; knowingly and intentionally making misrepresentations to plaintiff that induced plaintiff to transfer over $____ to defendants in ____ separate wire transactions; and by repeatedly making false statements designed to conceal defendants' fraud. Defendant Z

further misused and disclosed plaintiff's confidential and proprietary business information as part of his improper and fraudulent conduct, thereby breaching his fiduciary duties to his employer. Defendant Z's breach of fiduciary duties was intentional and malicious.

34. As a proximate result of Defendant Z's conduct plaintiff has suffered damages in an amount within the jurisdictional limits of this Court.
35. Plaintiff further seeks punitive damages, a constructive trust, and injunctive relief as set forth herein. Defendant Z represented to plaintiff verbally, in correspondence, and through the submission of fabricated bills of sale, invoices, and promissory notes that the corporate defendants were providing thousands of widgets to dealers with whom plaintiff had preexisting business relationships.
36. The corporate defendants benefited from Defendant Z's fraudulent representations by receiving the money wrongly obtained from plaintiff and upon information and belief had knowledge of the fraud and thus are vicariously liable for the fraud. Defendant Z's representations to plaintiff were material because they caused plaintiff to finance the corporate defendants' purported widget transactions with Dealer DL by transferring not less than $xx million to the defendants' bank accounts.
37. Defendant Z's material representations to plaintiff were false statements of fact, as widget dealers had no relationship whatsoever with the corporate defendants and the corporate defendants never provided any widgets to those dealers. Defendant Z concealed the fraudulent scheme by repeatedly making oral and written misrepresentations to his former

colleagues, supervisors, and other plaintiff representatives that the dealers had repaid the loans and that plaintiff had simply deposited the purported payments into the wrong accounts.

38. For example, Defendant Z represented to several colleagues that Dealer DL had repaid the loan it received to obtain widgets from Factory XYZ. In fact, Factory XYZ was not and is not in the business of distributing widgets. For its part, Dealer DL never received any widgets from Factory XYZ, was not familiar with Factory XYZ and never accepted a loan or repaid the loan for the transactions in question.
39. As another example, Defendant Z wrote in emails to several colleagues that he had received copies of the checks and check numbers that Dealer DL sent to plaintiff in repayment of the loan it received to obtain used widgets from Factory XYZ. In fact, Dealer DL never sent any checks to plaintiff in connection with any transaction with Factory XYZ.
40. In yet another example, Defendant Z created a document in 20____ that purported to set forth the steps he took to ensure that Dealer DL paid back the loans it supposedly received from plaintiff to purchase widgets from Factory XYZ. Defendant Z included in that document a list of individuals whom he purportedly contacted as part of his efforts to locate the funds. In fact, there was no loan and no repayment. Further, the individuals listed in that document did not speak to defendant and have no connection to the business.
41. Defendant Z made these representations to plaintiff knowing they were false and with the intent that plaintiff would rely on them in transferring no less than $xx million to the corporate defendants.

42. Plaintiff justifiably and actually relied on Defendant Z's material, fraudulent misrepresentations, believing them to be true, when it transferred funds into defendants' bank accounts to which defendants were not entitled.
43. Defendant Z's false representations directly and proximately caused injury to plaintiff, in the amount of not less than $XX million, plus interest, costs, and fees.
44. Upon information and belief, plaintiff's funds continue to be held in accounts or safety deposit boxes controlled by or for the benefit of the defendants.
45. By reason of defendants' actions, plaintiff has been, and will continue to be, seriously and irreparably damaged. Accordingly, plaintiff seeks injunctive relief as set forth herein and below preventing defendants and persons acting in concert with them from transferring or absconding with the money they have taken and any proceeds or other assets acquired with plaintiff's fund.
46. Plaintiff was fraudulently induced by defendants to transfer not less than $xx million into defendants' bank accounts. Defendant Z represented to plaintiff that the corporate defendants had provided or would provide widgets to Dealer DL. In fact, corporate defendants were not widget dealers, the corporate defendants did not sell widgets to Dealer DL, and defendants were not entitled to not less than $xx million they fraudulently obtained from plaintiff. Additionally, defendants wrongfully obtained and received money that, in equity and good conscience, belongs to plaintiff.

47. Plaintiff has attempted to recover the not less than $xx million that defendants owe plaintiff by filing suit and obtaining a temporary restraining order freezing the assets in defendants' bank accounts on 20___. Plaintiff has learned, however, that a substantial amount of plaintiff's funds transferred into defendants' bank accounts were moved to other accounts, at least some of which are controlled by defendants.
48. Accordingly, to date, plaintiff has failed to recover the funds owed to it by defendants.
49. Since approximately 20___, defendants fraudulently induced plaintiff into transferring approximately $xx million into defendants' bank accounts—funds to which defendants were not entitled. Defendants thereby became justly indebted to plaintiff in the amount of approximately $xx million.
50. Since at least 20___, Defendant Z solicited and accepted sums from his former colleagues and other individuals to pursue what Defendant Z described to them as special investment opportunities. As part of this arrangement, these individuals would wire or write personal checks for thousands, tens of thousands, or even hundreds of thousands of dollars to Defendant Z. In turn, Defendant Z promised these individuals that they would receive back their initial investment, interest, and a return. For a period of time, Defendant Z followed through on these promises. Defendant Z paid certain of these individuals with the funds he and the other defendants fraudulently received from plaintiff. Upon information and belief, Defendant Z currently owes these individuals

over $xxx million. Accordingly, an order freezing $xxx million of defendants' funds is insufficient to make plaintiff whole.

51. As a result, plaintiff likely will not be able to recover the approximately $xx million debt owed by defendants unless the writ of attachment is issued against Defendant Z.
52. Defendants wrongfully and fraudulently hold not less than $xxx million of plaintiff's funds in their bank accounts and other accounts controlled by them, which in equity and good conscience belongs to plaintiff.
53. Defendants have been and continue to be unjustly enriched by their possession of plaintiff's funds, having bestowed no benefit to plaintiff or Dealer DL, in return for the receipt of plaintiff's funds.
54. By reason of defendants' actions, plaintiff has been, and will continue to be, seriously and irreparably damaged.
55. Plaintiff has been injured by being deprived of its property by defendants. In contrast, defendants have been unjustly enriched by being allowed to retain and use plaintiff's funds.
56. Plaintiff has no adequate remedy at law to compensate it for the damage caused by defendants' actions. Accordingly, plaintiff is entitled to a constructive trust over the funds in defendants' bank accounts and all other accounts into which funds from these principal accounts flowed.
57. Plaintiff has no adequate remedy at law to compensate it for the damage caused by defendants' actions.
58. Plaintiff seeks the remedy of constructive trust in connection with all counts in this complaint.

Appendix B

Sample Affirmative Defenses and Counterclaims in a Constructive Trust Case

The following is intended as general guidance; there are few cases in which every single one of these would fit.

AS AND FOR A FIRST AFFIRMATIVE DEFENSE

1. There is a defense based on laches.
2. The plaintiff unreasonably delayed in filing this action.
3. Based on plaintiff's delay in seeking relief, defendant suffered prejudice.
4. Prejudice suffered by defendant due to the delay in plaintiff seeking relief includes that defendant was forced to enter a mortgage agreement on or about ____ and a promissory note dated on or about ____,

obligating defendant to pay the lender certain sums as indicated by those documents.

5. There has been a loss of potential evidence due to the plaintiff's unreasonable delay in seeking relief. This includes without limitation the following evidence ______. In addition, because of the delay, certain potential witnesses, including _______, became unavailable or died, causing a disadvantage to defendant in attempting to defend himself in this action.
6. Plaintiff inexplicably waited at least XX years after he transferred the premises located at _______ ("Premises") to defendant, and at least __ years after defendant took out a mortgage on the Premises located at _______ (the "Premises"), before filing this action.

AS AND FOR A SECOND AFFIRMATIVE DEFENSE

7. Plaintiff is equitably estopped from claiming a constructive trust.
8. Prejudice suffered by defendant due to the delay in plaintiff seeking relief includes that defendant was forced to enter a mortgage agreement on or about ____ and a promissory note dated on or about ____, obligating defendant to pay the lender certain sums as indicated by those documents. In addition, defendant did pay, over the past ____ years, the sum of at least ___ to the lender.
9. Prejudice suffered by defendant due to the delay in plaintiff seeking relief includes that defendant was repaired and renovated the Premises at costs of over $____.

AS AND FOR A THIRD AFFIRMATIVE DEFENSE

10. There is a defense based on waiver.
11. By taking the following actions, ________ and transferring the Premises to defendant pursuant to a deed, the plaintiff waived any claim of right to the Premises.
12. The plaintiff also orally waived any claim of right to the Premises.
13. The waivers described above took place on or about ____.

AS AND FOR A FOURTH AFFIRMATIVE DEFENSE

14. The plaintiff failed to name necessary parties, including, without limitation, the tenants of the Premises, and mortgagees of the Premises.
15. The plaintiff also failed to name potential beneficiaries to an alleged constructive trust, including the following persons ____________________ and/or the estate of the late ________ , who would potentially claim an interest in the alleged trust, for the following reasons: ________.

AS AND FOR A FIFTH AFFIRMATIVE DEFENSE

16. There is a defense based on the statute of frauds.
17. Despite the manner in which plaintiff's claim is pleaded, plaintiff's actual claim concerns an alleged oral agreement for the purchase of real property.
18. The alleged "agreement" concerns real property, was not in writing, and was not signed by defendant.

19. Plaintiff cannot enforce this so-called oral "agreement."
20. Alternatively the statute of frauds bars the claim because plaintiff's claim is based on alleged oral agreements in conflict with a written and signed agreement.

AS AND FOR A SIXTH AFFIRMATIVE DEFENSE

21. There is a defense based on the doctrine of judicial estoppel.
22. Plaintiff represented to the federal bankruptcy court, via sworn statement, in a proceeding entitled ____ or otherwise, that he had no interest in the Premises.
23. In that proceeding, due in part to that claim, plaintiff obtained a judgment in his benefit, discharging debts.

AS AND FOR A SEVENTH AFFIRMATIVE DEFENSE

24. There is a defense based on the doctrine of unclean hands.
25. In the event the parties engaged in the agreement described by plaintiff, then plaintiff sole reason for transferring the Premises was for the purposes of bank fraud or other fraud, including without limitation to obtain a mortgage on the Premises that plaintiff would not qualify for.
26. In the event the parties engaged in the agreement described by plaintiff, then plaintiff's sole reason for transferring the Premises was for the purposes of avoiding actual or potential creditors from seeking or obtaining relief against plaintiff.

27. In the event the parties engaged in the agreement described by plaintiff, then plaintiff's sole reason for transferring the Premises was for the purposes of avoiding paying government entities or the IRS with sums that plaintiff was obligated to pay.

AS AND FOR AN EIGHTH AFFIRMATIVE DEFENSE

28. There is a defense based on acquiescence and ratification.
29. The plaintiff was aware of, and permitted defendant to operate, control, pay expenses on, repair, and renovate the Premises over a period of ____ years.
30. The plaintiff failed to object to defendant's operation, control of, repairs or, or renovations to, the Premises.

AS AND FOR A NINTH AFFIRMATIVE DEFENSE

31. There is a defense based on the statute of limitations.
32. The plaintiff transferred the premises to defendant in ____.
33. The defendant took out mortgages on the Premises between ____ and ____.
34. Defendant implicitly or expressly disclaimed that plaintiff has any interest in the Premises more than six (6) years before this action was filed.
35. As such, the time for plaintiff to seek his constructive trust claim has elapsed.

AS AND FOR A TENTH AFFIRMATIVE DEFENSE

36. Money damages would suffice and fully compensate plaintiff for the alleged injuries he sustained.

AS AND FOR AN ELEVENTH AFFIRMATIVE DEFENSE

37. The transfer of the Premises from plaintiff to defendant was intended as a gift.

AS AND FOR A TWELFTH AFFIRMATIVE DEFENSE

38. There is a defense based on unjust enrichment.
39. Defendant made significant improvements on the Premises, and which increased in value due to the efforts of defendant. To allow plaintiff to obtain a constructive trust over the Premises would result in plaintiff's unjust enrichment

AS AND FOR A THIRTEENTH AFFIRMATIVE DEFENSE

40. Defendant provided full consideration for the Premises, including without limitation by providing funds to plaintiff, providing commercial space at no cost to plaintiff, and paying off debts of the plaintiff.

AS AND FOR A FOURTEENTH AFFIRMATIVE DEFENSE

41. The plaintiff and defendant entered into a written contract concerning the transfer of the Premises to defendant.
42. Because there is a written contract between the parties, the plaintiff is not permitted to claim unjust enrichment, which is a crucial element for a tort based on a constructive trust.

AS AND FOR A FIFTEENTH AFFIRMATIVE DEFENSE

43. The plaintiff lacks standing.
44. The plaintiff was not the previous owner of the Premises, prior to defendant obtaining a title interest.
45. If there were a constructive trust, the beneficiaries would be ____, rather than the plaintiff, as if defendant is unjustly enriched, only those parties would have a potential constructive trust.

AS AND FOR A FIRST COUNTERCLAIM

46. Defendant made significant improvements and renovations to the Premises.
47. Defendant paid significantly toward the balances of liens or mortgages against the Premises.
48. Defendant has consistently paid property taxes in connection with the Premises, and paid for insurance costs.
49. As a result of defendant's efforts, the Premises has increased in value.
50. Defendant is entitled to a money judgment for (1) any and all improvements and investments he made related to the premises, (2) the funds contributed toward the balance of the subject mortgages, and (3) the increase in property value, in an amount equal to at least $____,000,000.

AS AND FOR A SECOND COUNTERCLAIM

51. Defendant is entitled to an equitable lien in the Premises for (1) any and all improvements and investments he made related to the premises, (2) the

funds contributed toward the balance of the subject mortgages, and (3) the increase in property value, in an amount equal to at least $____,000,000.

AS AND FOR A THIRD COUNTERCLAIM

52. In the event plaintiff is granted any requested relief, defendant is entitled to an order compelling the plaintiff to pay off any balance in connection with any of the mortgages against the Premises.

Appendix C

Deposition Issues

A. Conducting Depositions

Although many attorneys do not do so in depositions, generally attorneys are permitted to ask adversary witnesses leading questions.[1] As a matter of style, during depositions, since there are many unknowns, it would not make sense to make every question a leading one. However, when it comes to the most critical issues, one might consider using leading questions for those matters, especially after a round of questions that touches on a particular issue.

The following are sample leading questions one might consider asking. Some of the questions are obvious, but to paraphrase Sherlock Holmes, the world is full of obvious questions which nobody by any chance ever asks.

1. *See, e.g.*, CAL. EVID. CODE § 767, subd. (a) (2); GAB Business Services, Inc. v. Moore, 829 S.W.2d 345, 351 (Tex. App. 1992); Galvin v. Hinkle, 2004 N.Y. Slip Op. 30342, 5 (N.Y. Sup. Ct. 2004); TEX. R. CIV. EVID. 611(b).

Statute of Limitations

Questions to ask of the plaintiff and alleged donor.

You were aware you transferred the property to defendant in 2010?

And you knew as of 2012 that defendant would refuse to return it?

But you waited to file this lawsuit until 2020?

And this was even though he told you in specific in 2012 that he was going to keep it?

And you waited because you had many other things going on in your life, so it just took you some time to retain counsel, right?

Questions to ask of the defendant and alleged trustee.

You never actually told the plaintiff what you intended to do with the property right?

You never formally informed him that you would keep the property forever, did you?

After all, you had no reason to contact him about your intentions for the property; at the time, you were doing your own thing with it, correct?

Relationship

Questions to ask of the plaintiff and alleged donor.

You do not trust the defendant, right?

He's not a trustworthy person, correct?

And even before you transferred him the property, you were already suspicious of him, weren't you?

There were many hints that he could not be trusted, even before you transferred him the property.

The fact that he refused to transfer it to you is not a surprise, right?

And that's because even when you transferred it to him, you knew there was a real chance he wouldn't return it to you.

You would not say you had a close relationship to him before the transfer right?

You never went to him for advice?

Questions to ask of the defendant and alleged trustee.

You were quite close?

You lived together for __ years?

You grew up together? Ate meals together?

He had good reason to trust you, right?

You never did anything to make him distrust you?

Unclean Hands

Questions to ask of the plaintiff and alleged donor.

When you transferred the property to defendant, that was because you had creditors seeking to collect money from you, right?

And you thought this would be a good way to make sure they couldn't collect the funds from you directly?

When you transferred the property to defendant, you knew you wouldn't qualify for a mortgage, right?

So you told defendant to put it in his name, and therefore you could find a way to get the mortgage, without the bank knowing it was actually your property, right?

Questions to ask of the defendant and alleged trustee.

You told the plaintiff that you wanted him to do this, and why you wanted him to do it, right?

You were not harmed by what the plaintiff did, were you? It only helped you, correct?

And in fact you were the one who suggested he go about it this way, correct?

Transfer

Questions to ask of the plaintiff and alleged donor.

You never actually transferred the property to defendant—you just gave him money periodically, right?

And this was monthly?

And the sum you provided, wouldn't that be approximately the same amount one might expect to give as rent for the portion of the premises you were living in?

Questions to ask of the defendant and alleged trustee.

You received payments from the plaintiff—correct?

And those payments were connected to plaintiff's ownership of the property?

If you're calling it "rent" then you of course had no lease agreement with him, did you? Or at least none in writing?

And normally rent does not go up and down—it stays the same, right? But in this case, the plaintiff provided funds at varying amounts, correct?

Mistake

Questions to ask of the plaintiff and alleged donor.

What was the original understanding between the parties?

When you transferred the property to defendant, you did not actually specify that he would have to give it back right?

If that's your claim that you made it specific, why not put it in writing?

You know how to write words in English, right?

No one told you not to write down your deal, right?

You just weren't in the mood to get out a piece of paper, right?

But this property is worth $xxx,000, right?

And you just decided not to write down even one word of explanation about why you might get it back. Is that what you're saying?

And that's because you decided it wasn't worth your effort to write down a few sentences on a piece of paper, right?

Questions to ask of the defendant and alleged trustee.

There was no logical reason the plaintiff would have had to transfer the property to you?

You were probably surprised when he did so, right?

You don't have any documents indicating that this was his intention, do you?

Whether the Transfer Was a Gift

Questions to ask of the plaintiff and alleged donor.

You understand that relatives sometimes give each other gifts, right?

And you have probably given relatives gifts sometimes, right?

And they have given you gifts too, right?

And when you give gifts, you don't put anything in writing about it—you just give it.

And that's what happened here too—you transferred something to defendant, and did not put anything in writing about it.

Questions to ask of the defendant and alleged trustee.

Are you claiming this was a gift?

But you didn't do anything special for him to warrant this gift?

And the giver didn't announce this in front of anyone?

And the giver had other relatives and friends, but somehow you wound up with this?

And he never explained why everyone else in the family should be cut out, and that only you would get this?

And there's no logical explanation for that either, right?

B. Defending Depositions

"Boxer could not get beyond the letter D. He would trace out A, B, C, D, in the dust with his great hoof, and then would stand staring at the letters with his ears back, sometimes shaking his forelock, trying with all his might to remember what came next and never succeeding. On several occasions, indeed, he did learn E, F, G, H, but by the time he knew them, it was always discovered that he had forgotten A, B, C, and D."

—George Orwell, *Animal Farm*

Sometimes it is tempting to give one's client a great deal of instructions on how to prepare for a deposition, but many clients cannot handle it. It may be a once in a lifetime experience, and they will be best off with just a few instructions. Some of the most crucial ones are:

- Keep the answers short, without going into issues that the attorney did not ask about.
- Do not explain anything, unless asked to. If it helps, you can remind your client of the old adage "Never apologize; never explain."
- Pause and think before you speak.

If you are advising a nonparty in defending a deposition, the most critical advice one can give is to tell that nonparty to tell the truth, and then you can tell him "If they ever ask you what advice I gave you, tell them I told you to tell the truth." Then if that question comes up, that response will often end the topic. You will look more honest than Abraham Lincoln and George Washington, combined.

For advanced clients, an attorney might be tempted to give them advice about how to delay, give non-answers, or to otherwise frustrate the questioner. This book will not explain how to give that kind of advice. That, as President Nixon said, "would be wrong."

In particular for a constructive trust case, at the very least, the client should be alerted to the crucial areas that are in dispute, such as the relationship between the parties, the circumstances constituting the wrong, and potential statute of limitation defenses. One solid method is to meet with one's client days ahead of time, and give sample questions of the most potentially damning questions.

Index